# No One Is
# Self-Made

# No One Is Self-Made

## BUILD YOUR VILLAGE TO FLOURISH IN BUSINESS AND LIFE

## Dr. Lakeysha Hallmon

**DEY**ST.
*An Imprint of* William Morrow

**DEY**ST.

FIRST EDITION

*Chapter opener illustration © Cienpies Design/stock.adobe.com*

Library of Congress Cataloging-in-Publication Data has been applied for.

ISBN 978-0-06-331589-1

24 25 26 27 28  LBC  5 4 3 2 1

To my beloved mother and father, Carolyn and Roger. Though you reign with the ancestors, my dear mother, I see you in everything beautiful and feel you at every sunrise. Thank you for always believing in me, for always being my first audience, and for knowing that one day I would write my first book. Daddy, every time I call you, you pick up, and every time, I am assured that I am a well-loved Black woman. To my grandparents, Henry (RIP) and Josephine Hallmon, as well as Huria Lee (RIP) and Bobbie Smith, thank you for every sacrifice you made that allowed me the freedom to write this book. To my siblings, Yolanda, Roderick, and Whitney, I love you all so much. To my nephews, Sean, Amir, and Jaxon, may you always believe in the power of the village. All that I do, I do for you. I love you in and out of time. Lastly, I dedicate this book to every entrepreneur and change agent who dreams of building differently and who are creating villages.

# CONTENTS

# No One Is
# Self-Made

# Introduction

I AM NOT SURE WHERE YOU ARE IN YOUR ENTREPRENEURIAL journey. You may already be working toward a higher goal—something bigger than yourself that enriches not only your life but the lives of the people to your left and right—and are seeking extra guidance. Perhaps you have felt stirrings that there is something more meaningful than simply turning a profit or amassing followers, and you are searching for purpose, for that full-body yes feeling that signals you are on the right path. Maybe you are at a crossroads where you must make a big decision about your business and are unsure of which direction to take. Or you might feel stuck or unsettled, like the matrix is off somehow. Some of you might even be feeling defeated, having experienced one too many rejections; maybe you're thinking entrepreneurial success isn't meant for you. Perhaps you are burned out and are considering an exit strategy. I have been at each of these precipices and have eventually found my footing, oftentimes after a slip—and sometimes because of it.

Wherever you find yourself—ideation phase, start-up, scaling, pivoting—I want you to trust this: The right community works. When the right community is baked in at every stage of your business building, you cannot go off the rails. As an entrepreneur, you are in a position to shift your village and world. Not just *your* world but *the* world. How you do business, from the smallest transaction to the big-picture moves, lays down a blueprint that can either set you and your business up for sustainable, healthy, communal success or lead you down a different road, one that replicates the inequitable systems that prize personal wealth over giving those on the margins the opportunity to thrive. You are modeling how to exist in the world.

AS A CHILD, my favorite place to be during summer break was huddled underneath my grandmother's sewing machine, peeking out as her customers put in their orders for school uniforms, work uniforms, and choir robes. My grandmother's tiny town of Marks, Mississippi, sat on the edge of the Mississippi Delta. It was the starting point of the 1968 Mule Train, a campaign of poverty awareness, and the birthplace of the Blues Highway (Highway 61), a live-music blues crawl that follows the route Black people took to Chicago during the Great Migration. Though rich with a beautiful culture and people, Marks lies in the most economically distressed corner of the most economically distressed state, home to one of the highest Black populations in the United States. There was very little in the way of work prospects, which were mostly limited to cotton field labor. So my grandmother decided to become a seamstress to bring in money for herself and her family.

Above the humming of the sewing machine with its rhythmic whir, I heard her greet her customers by name. I remember Mr. Hank, a friendly plumber, who needed a new work uniform. Mrs. Grimes and Mrs. Burnett, teachers sorting out their school-year wardrobe, came in for skirts, slacks, and dresses to be taken in or let out. I listened as they caught up on neighborhood news and soothed one another when that news was bad. My grandmother—Bobbi Jean to her friends and Mrs. Bobbi to everyone else—was warm with all her clients and also extremely focused and hardworking, priding herself on exemplary work. I watched her foot pump the pedal of the machine and shift the fabric as she guided it precisely under the needle as it moved up and down. I was fascinated by the process, but mostly I stayed near her because I loved her. I felt protected sitting at her feet, surrounded by her brightly colored sewing tools—her yellow tape measure, the red tomato-shaped pincushion with the colorful pins, her silver thimble. I felt a part of something larger, safe, and welcoming.

I watched as her business grew in tandem with her community; I saw how her gifts benefited her customers and how her customers supported her business. My grandmother began creating more complicated patterns as her skills blossomed and her community members' lives unfolded, requiring new outfits to mark new milestones—bridal gowns for weddings and suits and dresses for graduations and special church events. It felt like a tight-knit village, one where folks had each other's backs, materially, economically, and emotionally.

Looking back, I can see that my grandmother and her business planted early seeds in my mind about the power of community and how it intersects with purpose, a calling that uses a person's gifts for the betterment of the village. Within a town where opportunities were limited, she had found a way to embrace her gifts and the talents handed down by her late mother, who also sewed, in order to serve her community and rely on them at the same time. I didn't know it then, but her work would inspire my own entrepreneurial journey, one that would culminate in the Village Market, the company I founded to create economic parity for Black entrepreneurs in Atlanta and beyond.

Community as a construct wasn't on my radar until the early 2000s, when I attended the National Black Arts Festival in Atlanta at Underground Atlanta, an outdoor mall and entertainment district that I had been advised was a cultural experience. I'd made the trip from Mississippi (where I was teaching) to explore graduate school options, and what I saw took my breath away. There were Black painters, Black sculptors, Black designers, all sharing space while simultaneously showcasing the diversity of what it meant to be Black. I'd never seen anything like it. I'd enjoyed thriving marketplaces before—browsing the wares, hearing the artisans and customers laughing, connecting to my fellow humans in a way I could never feel in a suburban mall. But suddenly I was struck by the fact that I had little to no identity in those places. As much as I'd felt welcomed in other places, I never had that feeling of being home. But here I saw myself, my family, my village. A whisper was telling me that Atlanta, the home of many civil rights icons and Black pioneers, was where I needed to be. I didn't recognize it then, but I was feeling the glimmer of what would become one of my purposes.

I moved to Atlanta in 2011. In Mississippi, I'd been an English teacher for nearly half a decade, which I loved, but I was thrilled to move to a city with such a vibrant and rich Black history. Soon after my arrival, I became an evaluation and research specialist with the Georgia Department of Education (GADOE), training teachers and superintendents in social and emotional learning and improving after-school programs. When I wasn't on any site visits, I'd pack up my computer and head to either Drip or Urban Grind, local coffee shops where I could work. As soon as I had set up my laptop, I'd say good morning to whoever was sitting near me and, as a sometimes extrovert, I'd really mean it, which made them say good morning back and really mean it too. Before long, I was making friends, learning about their lives and what they were hoping to achieve.

Over time I became friendly with Urban Grind's owner, Cassandra, an entrepreneur who'd intentionally created a community in her neighborhood through her business. I also got to know many patrons from the coffee shops that I frequented. Among them were a talented and eclectic part-time DJ, a soulful baker trying to open his own shop, and a determined guy starting an insurance company without a brick-and-mortar space, who savvily suggested "meeting for coffee" with potential customers. I was inspired by the level of creativity and drive of these ambitious entrepreneurs who were chasing their passions. As a curious person, I started asking questions: Why is this something you do only on the side? How do you target customers? I pressed on with some big-goal questions, my gi-ant imagination dreaming for them. From my DJ friend, I wanted to know how people got contracts with hotels and how DJ parties were managed for big events. More often than not, my new friends didn't have all the answers. They were still figuring these things out themselves.

At the same time, I began to understand more about the racial disparities in the local small-business economy. The researcher in me was curious about whether the challenges of my coffee-shop community were part of a larger pattern. What I discovered was dis-heartening: Only 4 percent of Black businesses survive the start-up phase, and Black businesses in Atlanta have an average value of only $58,000—eleven times less than white-owned businesses. What was at the root of this huge gap in a city that is deemed the Black mecca? Many things, as it turns out: difficulty establishing business credit and securing business loans, not having enough capital to launch and expand, not being able to set up shop in locations with pedes-trian traffic, to name just a few. Many of these deficits, I discovered, were tied to decades of a widening racial wealth gap, a chasm that has made it nearly impossible for Black households everywhere (not just in Atlanta) to build generational wealth—those assets like homes and investments that are passed along to children and grand-children. Compared to white households, whose wealth has been growing over decades, Black households' wealth has dropped. White households hold more than ten times the wealth of Black households. My new friends, most of whom were Black, were all facing the same economic struggles, no matter their industry, and were trying to make it independently within a system that wasn't set up for their success. They were making a go of it, with fantastic products, services, and passion, but they lacked support and resources.

An idea began to take root in my head, one stoked by the beau-tiful art and artists I had seen years earlier at the National Black

Arts Festival and fueled by one of the truest things about me: I was a teacher. Atlanta's Black entrepreneurial community needed someone who could connect those who needed answers with those who had the answers. That stirring I'd felt years earlier returned and was urging me to gather the people in my little village, folks who were already living in alignment with their purpose and those who were on the road to figuring themselves out.

I envisioned a speaker series where successful Black entrepreneurs would share their stories to educate and lift up this community that was becoming so important to me. With the support of Cassandra, it came together. In January of 2016, the first It Takes a Village Speaker Series was held at Urban Grind, one of the oldest Black woman–owned coffee shops in Atlanta. In the spirit of a village, everyone in attendance had two obligations: First, each person was required to support Cassandra by purchasing at least two things from the coffee shop; and second, everyone had to promise to share what they learned at the event with someone in their community. The speakers were simply required to tell the truth, to share their lived experience—the successes and the stumbles—and help perpetuate success in the Black entrepreneur community.

The first event had seventy-six people. By the second one, there was a line outside the door. I followed up with six more events. At each gathering, I marveled as I watched people engaging in spirited conversation and swapping tips and phone numbers. And Cassandra saw a spike in sales—especially important because a popular chain coffee shop had just opened a couple doors down.

I was thrilled. But I was also experiencing a growing frustration. The more I witnessed the talent and passion of my village of entrepreneurs, the more I began to notice the lack of Black presence in the festivals and markets I attended around Atlanta. There was clearly a whole pocket of talented entrepreneurs who didn't get the invite, and their products were just as nice as any of the sellers in front of me. Black entrepreneurs needed a spotlight, a way to connect with potential customers to expand their reach and grow their sales.

Fresh off my high from the speaker event, I thought: What if *I* built it? As a naturally creative person, I had always allowed myself to dream about what could exist. Since I was young, I conjured up loving and amazing futures for myself and my family, trusting that some version of my dreams would materialize. As a young adult, I envisioned all sorts of projects and felt driven to bring them to life. Now, faced with an obvious community need and a growing sense of purpose to help fulfill it, I let my imagination unfurl. It would be a market filled with Black entrepreneurs, a place of bustling productivity, joy, and diversity that would lift up everyone in the Black community. I jotted down some ideas and diagrams on a piece of paper to help shape it, as I've found there is power in writing things down. I allowed my vision to expand: There would also be a business incubator to accelerate promising Black entrepreneurs and a vibrant space where patrons could meet and support these incredible business owners. It would be a place where solopreneurs could build their confidence and find the material and social resources to go after their dreams, to build businesses with a collective mindset. If they faltered, they would have a net to catch them and a village to raise them back up again. They would all be succeeding together, sharing the wins, learning from the stumbles, and being in relationship with one another in ways that prioritized collaboration, not competition. The Village Market began to form in my mind. I mulled over the idea for a few short months. It kept tugging at me until it was undeniable. By the time the fourth speaker series came around, my idea was crystallized, as certain as anything surrounding me in the real world. That evening, I tested the waters, posing a question to the room: "Who here could be ready in six weeks to introduce their products and services to *a lot* of customers?" Multiple hands shot up. I had my answer.

I had zero experience in the entrepreneurial space. I had never booked an event space. I didn't know how I was supposed to find parking lot attendants. I had no understanding of permits or sponsors. All I knew was that I was envisioning what was needed, that this was the way toward something better for the Black community, that I was the person who was going to do it, and that I would find and meet the people who would help me get there. I got to work, leaning on my tribe of friends for support. I did what I was trained to do: research and learn and connect. I worked my connections and reached out to those whom I hoped would have answers. I read everything I could get my hands on. By day, I was an educator; by night and on weekends, I became a blossoming entrepreneur myself, intent on creating the ultimate gathering place for exceptional Black entrepreneurs. What I did not do was strive to build this completely on my own. I had never bought into the myth of self-made. Nor was it a goal of mine. I knew that in order to build this village, I'd want and need the support of "my village."

The first Village Market took place in April 2016 at the Defoor Center, an event space in the upper west side of Atlanta. Our tagline: *We Gather, We Circulate, We Celebrate.* It was everything I envisioned and more, and it was the essence of a village—entrepreneurs, many of them from the speaker series, supporting one another; patrons excited to shop; and everyone joyously engaging in the experience. It was important to me that the event, while evocative of a marketplace, not be confused with a casual flea market—I made sure it felt elegant and curated, an evening event with tables covered with black linen. Our focus that night was to spend locally, to circulate money in the community. I wanted people to understand that we were all in that room to *do* something. This wasn't just a cool event for selfies. I had studied group economics and cooperatives in college, ways of running businesses that center the collective and intentionally keep money flowing within that community. Nearly 50 percent of each purchase at local independent businesses is recirculated locally, compared to less than 14 percent of purchases at chain stores. Local, intentional, group economics has been responsible for the survival of communities, especially Black communities, throughout history, from O. W. Gurley's Black Wall Street in the early 1900s, a model of community determination and economic resilience and power, to similar communities in Durham, North Carolina; Wilmington, Delaware; and Mound Bayou, Mississippi. I wanted the Village Market to be a continuation of that work, a nod to those who came before us, an ancestral pull that would keep us going.

And it was. Everything about that night—the collaboration, the intentionality, the joy, and the economic impact—felt like divine alignment. This was what I was supposed to be doing.

What started out as a desire to help my friends create successful businesses—to spend money in the community, to make the support tangible and spread the love—burst into something bigger. Several things, actually. Over the next four years, my team and I curated dozens of marketplaces—focusing on the inclusion of kid-preneurs, holistic products, and plant-based foods—to introduce excellent Black businesses into the ecosystem, strengthening the entire community. I pulled in sponsors and created merchandise to fuel our "Support Is a Verb" campaign, an initiative meant to emphasize action—the *doing*—as the engine for community prosperity. During the pandemic, I pivoted and opened the Village Retail, a brick-and-mortar shopping space at the Ponce City Market, which boasts the second-highest foot traffic in the city. Yes, I was gutsy enough (some would say crazy!) to open up a physical store during the pandemic. But I believed so profoundly in human connection and community— something we were all desperately lacking during those endless socially distanced years with interminable Zooms and a reliance on social media—that I knew it would not only work but that it would thrive. To ensure it was sustainable for the long haul, I borrowed

ideas from group economics, collectively pooling resources to accomplish together what would be difficult (or impossible) to achieve
alone. I intentionally took steps away from capitalism, which I believe furthers inequities and isolation, and instead wove inclusive
values and equitable economic practices into my model. In 2020, I
founded my nonprofit, Our Village United, as a way to deepen the
mission of the business, offering grants, technical assistance, small-
business development programming open to the public, and a business incubator to mentor fledgling Black entrepreneurs. We have
since developed partnerships with Target, Mastercard, Walmart, the
Rockefeller Foundation, the W. K. Kellogg Foundation, and celebrity
foundations, like the Jordan Brand, to elevate promising Black entrepreneurs.

None of this was easy. Any entrepreneur who has built anything
worthwhile knows this. Many days, I experienced multiple nos, including blatant dismissals and even a harsh "Black-focused ventures
are a trend that won't last." To state the obvious, the capitalist systems in this country that work well for the wealthy and connected
and white do not always benefit people of color or those without
family wealth. It was designed this way—banking, real estate, commerce in this country were mostly built by white men for white men,
a game created by them to be played by them. I've always known
this on some level, but it wasn't until I began to build my business
from the ground up that I realized how contaminated the roots of
our nation's systems are. Black and Hispanic women in our country
get just 0.43 percent of the venture capital money—*less than half a
percent*—whereas white men get 93 percent. Those dismal numbers
reflect who is making decisions about which businesses get funding:
Only 1 percent of venture capitalists are Black (again, mostly men—
just 0.03 percent are Black women). In moments of my own doubt
and challenges, I've had to retreat and meditate, pray and trust that
the winding path was all connected to my purpose. I intentionally
tap into a mindset of abundance, one that assures there is enough for

us all and that rejects the idea of scarcity and hopelessness. Most of all, I trust that my people will show up when I need them to, that my community will light the way. I'm a very optimistic person, and my purpose in creating the Village Market, the Village Retail, and Our Village United is to change these dismal statistics by constructing a system that works for us because it *is* for us.

Today, the Village Market is a thriving umbrella organization dedicated to advancing Black-owned businesses. In all its iterations, we have showcased more than 1,400 Black businesses from thirty-eight states and two countries (Canada and the Bahamas), growing the community to embrace far-flung villagers from all over the country. We've generated more than $8 million for Black entrepreneurs across the country. My enterprises have also shifted the way we show up for one another. Employees and the business owners we support embrace a purpose-driven, community-first approach, one that respects individual roles and contributions but never at the expense of the collective. Doing business with an understanding that no one is self-made, that our playground for risk is safer and more prosperous when we carry one another, and that we are one another's salvation, has revealed itself to me as the *way forward*.

And I am not done building out the vision. There is much more to accomplish.

THE VILLAGE IS *an entrepreneur's most precious resource. The collective, where each person within that community sees the value of the mission and of one another, is the most sustainable business model for the Black community and for any community, for that matter.* The village blueprint is the surest way to live a purpose-fueled life and to achieve your wildest entrepreneurial dreams. It is the antidote to the widening racial wealth gap—for every $100 of white wealth, Black households hold just $15—and positions the next generation for success. When we share space and lift one another up, the collective shine is so much brighter than what we can achieve alone—and it allows everyone else to prosper as well.

While I firmly believe this is the most prosperous way to success for village-minded entrepreneurs, I understand that it comes with some misgivings. You may be concerned about whether you'll be able to survive, purchase a home or your first commercial real estate property, or give your children a life beyond what you experienced. You may be thinking, "If I bring in community, will it limit how far I can go?" I want to reassure you that both prosperity and community are possible. They are interconnected. I am an example of that. And we have many historical examples of how togetherness delivers us into shared abundance. The truth is that no one—and I mean *no one*—is self-made. This does not mean that hard work and determination and talent do not count, but the idea that anyone in our society has achieved wealth and success on their own is a myth, and a dangerous one at that. When we mythologize entertainers or unicorn entrepreneurs (people or businesses who seemingly skyrocket to epic success overnight) as self-made, we erase the narratives of the people who contributed to that person's rise, whether that assistance was emotional, financial, or structural. Building the stage is as important as standing on it. We live in a society that values individualism, but if we don't intentionally build connections and treat those relationships as our compass, we devalue our most cherished resource: one another.

Witnessing the hardships of Black and Brown people—environmental disasters, discriminatory economic and health-care policies, and the rescinding of affirmative action, to name a few—I am increasingly convinced that local support is a necessity: No one will step in to save you except for yourself, your neighbors, and your community. The solution to so many of our challenges comes down to a community-focused model. This is true for all Americans but particularly for Black Americans. Since Black people's forced arrival in the country, we have been subjected to inequities and inequalities meant to shatter our hope and aspirations. George Floyd's murder in 2020 was a tipping point: For nine minutes, the world watched his spirit seep from his body, his death causing one of the longest acts of protest and resistance that this country has ever experienced. Though Black people are resilient—we have the brilliance and mental and spiritual fortitude to persevere in spite of what we've been subjected to—we cannot do this effectively, or at all, separated and isolated from one another. Dr. Martin Luther King Jr. and the late Senator John Lewis spoke frequently of the return to "the beloved community." The only way Black people in our country have been able to thrive is by coming together in mutual support. Gathering and sourcing from our beloved community is how we can find the resources and trust to create the economic mobility and generational wealth that have been denied us for far too long. Beloved community catches us when we fall. It allows us to fall forward, not down, then pours into us the love and reserves we need to get back up. It heals us as we rise, for we are sharing the burdens along with the benefits.

When entrepreneurs build with the village model, success is achieved on all measures for both the community and the individuals who make up that community. The villagers in my orbit—in my business and nonprofit and in the entrepreneurs we touch through our work—are not intimidated by the success and talents of others but instead are motivated by them. They are actively giving *and* asking for help, engaging in real, tangible support. They are changing their relationship with money, understanding their own value and the importance of operating at their best. They embrace the fact that shared resources and information and support lead to abundance for everyone.

Leaders of these growing businesses are harnessing each person's unique role in service of the village mission and prioritizing the health of the relationships, which rests on the health of the individuals within the ecosystem. For this reason, everyone in the Village Market, the Village Retail, and Our Village United is learning to balance hard work with self-care. Instead of pushing too hard until we burn out or adopting toxic grind traits, we are embracing holistic modalities of self-care. By self-care, I am not referring to a luxurious spa vacation in Bali or lounging in pricey, pastel athleisure wear—that is the commercialization of self-care. Instead, I am talking about self-care that is accessible to everyone anywhere: taking breaks for deep breathing or a walk or complete stillness, going inward to meditate or just exist in your body, or connecting with your source and finding your version of rest and recharge (and no judgment if you have racked up miles going to Bali). You cannot build a well-functioning community—let alone be an optimal leader—if there is not intentional space and resources dedicated to the emotional, mental, and physical wellness of the individuals who are doing the work of a shared mission.

I came to these truths incrementally, over time. I believe that our life tasks and assignments, the breadcrumbs that point us toward our bigger purpose, are delivered in digestible doses so that we can savor the learnings and the lessons. Community is built in small rooms with intentional people, and it grows, gradually.

Being together in a healthy, loving village is important for all of us, no matter our race, religion, or gender, for it enables us to see the full humanity in one another and to act and lead with empathy. It is likely that we all have been in rooms where we've been dismissed or unfairly targeted. There have been moments where our humanity has been antagonized and our light dimmed. This is the opposite of a well community and a sign you are not where you are meant to be, that you are not with the people who are aligned with your purpose or values. It is a discomfort so strong that it will propel you to move on, to seek or even build your own well village. To state the obvious—because it still needs stating—Black people must be seen as fully human, because when we interact with police, judges, doctors, business owners, and others in power, our survival and outcomes depend on it. Structural racism places shackles on progress. While Black communities have developed a powerful resiliency in response to centuries of oppression, we owe it to ourselves and future generations to intentionally channel our energy into actions that fuel our collective mobility, to plug into the power source—the village—to supercharge progress. We gain everything by standing and unifying together. We gain everything by seeing one another. All communities can benefit from a village approach, but for the Black community, time is urgent, and that time is now. We must figure out what togetherness looks like as we build.

I wrote this book to support the beloved community of entrepreneurs that exists beyond the walls and spreadsheets and incubators of the Village Market. I am sharing my successes and failures to shine a light for those of you who have a desire to build differently and are in a position to affect change, to live and work together with purpose to change the world. This book is a rallying cry—your community needs you and the world needs you. This book is also for those of you who are unsure and untested, who want to try but are scared of failing. I've got you. Your village has got you.

I've designed this book's chapters as a journey, one that begins with a deep understanding that we are one another's harvest and that concludes at a juncture where you have all the tools and assurance you'll need to build differently, collectively, prosperously. In between, I'll challenge you to reflect on your mindset and your self-work and to explore your unique gifts and innate purpose in your business and community. I share ways to identify a dream team of value-aligned villagers and to create an environment that pours into the people at the heart of your mission. You'll be inspired to build with a mindset of shared prosperity and with equitable systems that prioritize the community without sacrificing profits. My great hope is that reading this will be an emotional and spiritual experience that leads to action and that empowers you to approach your work life and community building with an open mind and, more importantly, an open heart focused on collective upward mobility. It is the heart and intentional actions that can guide and drive change to advance and propel the community. But everything starts with the self. This book will drive you to become your best self so that you can show up fully in community.

> . . . we are each other's
> harvest:
> we are each other's
> business:
> we are each other's
> magnitude and bond.
> —GWENDOLYN BROOKS, "PAUL ROBESON," 1970

# ONE

# The Myth of Self-Made

"SELF-MADE" IS A MYTH.

Being self-made means that a person has achieved success or financial independence solely through their own efforts, often starting from humble beginnings and working hard to overcome obstacles and achieve one's goals rather than inheriting wealth or receiving significant help from others. It's a concept as American as blue jeans or football, the idea that with just hard work and motivation you can build anything on your own. We hear it as a through line in rap music; we see it in the glamorization of "unicorn" entrepreneurs and underdog stories fashioned by Hollywood.

But it's not *real*. The reality is that everyone receives some form of help, and that support comes in many forms—financial, emotional, mentorship, social. Of all the successful entrepreneurs I know and have read about, self-made isn't an accurate description for *any* of them. Everyone, no matter how seemingly independent and no matter how brilliant and hardworking, is a product of their village in some way. Success is built on community and collective efforts, but the myth of going it alone has saturated our culture. Which is why when someone describes me as self-made, I kindly redirect them: "Thank you, but I'm village-made."

To believe a person is self-made is not only fiction, it's harmful. When we subscribe to the idea that an individual can achieve wealth and success all on their own, we set up a false expectation for what is possible and what is endeavor-worthy. If we buy into the myth that the solo journey is somehow more honorable or achievable than a collaborative effort, we may end up shouldering unnecessary burdens and limiting our growth. We may be reluctant to ask for help—or we may outright reject it. If we do accept assistance, we may feel ashamed. A self-made mindset actually keeps people laboring alone and, in doing so, feeds burnout. We think that doing it on our own is what we have to do or that it's valiant. Believing a person succeeds solely on their individual merits also ignores the systemic barriers and inequalities that exist in society, the economic, racial, and gender-based disparities that push some people down while lifting others up. Expecting the individual to do it all excuses us from having to work toward creating a more equitable and just society.

When the idea of the Village Market grabbed me by the soul in 2016—when I stepped into my purpose of building a community-oriented business to elevate Black entrepreneurs in Atlanta, a city where Black businesses earn eleven times less than white-owned businesses—I understood that its success would necessitate gathering the village, working hard, and asking for and accepting help. By creating an event where the community was showing up and investing financially in the small businesses who were part of the village, and grounding it in the theme of "collaboration over competition," I knew that businesses would be more intrinsically motivated to reach a shared mission and that we'd keep money circulating locally. I felt certain that the people who would help bring my vision to fruition were close by and that with the community's support we'd all rise together. I'd seen the power and warmth of community since I was a child, watching my grandmother's sewing business flourish. As I began to envision the Village Market, I remembered the embraces, the laughter, and the safety of that time, and I knew that in order to actualize my vision, I had to build the village in such a way. I had to embrace a village mindset.

The very first thing I did, even before drawing up a business plan, was to lean on my group of friends. I excitedly shared with them my vision of the Village Market: a bustling and joyous and profitable quarterly marketplace filled with exceptional Black entrepreneurs who risked and stumbled and succeeded together. My little but mighty tribe jumped on board with my vision and immediately supported me by saying—and *meaning*—that whatever I needed, they'd be there, whether it was to work the door at the event, spread the word, or offer their skills as a DJ or marketer or numbers cruncher. Within my immediate family, I confided first in my older sister for moral support. Yolanda allows excitement to slowly simmer before she emotes. She listens and reflects, so I can rely on her response being authentic and measured and always with my best interests at heart. "Whatever you need, Sean [her son] and I are there," she told me. From that point on, I felt confident moving forward because I knew that if I fumbled, they would all be there to pick me up, to cheerlead and offer solutions. I do believe that to create something great you need intrinsic motivation, dedication, and drive as well as a commitment to learn and perfect, which I had in spades; but I also believe that encouragement from others provides fuel for your drive. Emotional support, while not as flashy as getting the big check, is an investment in you, one that can have an enormous impact.

Relying on others was the most viable option for success and it was a necessity. At the time, I was still working for the Georgia Department of Education (GADOE) as an evaluator for after-school programs in the state, so I couldn't devote as much time as I wanted to launch my business. I also had zero experience in the entrepreneurial space, so I reached out to those whom I hoped would have answers—people who had followed their vision and leaned on their villages to make it happen—trusting that they would offer their experience and wisdom to pave my path. A good friend with a successful insurance business shared with me that it would be important to start thinking about my mission statement right away so I could easily communicate my goals to others and stay focused on what mattered. He also suggested that I convince the community, and in particular the businesses in the community (my target market), to trust my model, which was somewhat outside the norm, as I was envisioning an experience that showcased nontoxic products—plant-based organic foods, apparel, candles, beverages, you name it—that celebrated Black culture. Part of my vision of a holistic marketplace involved introducing the community to the many things that I was also learning—the connection between nourishing food and health and intentional spending. I did not see this approach elsewhere in the community, and I felt it would be well received and impactful. Connecting one-on-one, I invited many local business owners to participate, letting them know my parameters and assuring them that everything was quality driven (I was, after all, an untested entrepreneur asking them to take a chance on me). Most importantly, I emphasized that at the center of it all was the wellness of the village, of Black entrepreneurs and the community they served.

Another friend, who had a wellness company, supported me by sharing her important must-haves. "Get a bookkeeper, start working on your trademark, create an operations process—who will be doing what and how will it be done?" she advised me. Although I couldn't afford all these things right away, I researched them and identified folks who might one day hold specific positions in the business, which was motivating and helped me build out my vision. She also gave me the best advice I received: *Take care of yourself in the process.* I already had a practice of meditating, working out, and eating healthfully, but the Village Market was quickly taking over my nights and weekends. As my business scaled, I struggled with balancing self-care and work. I would return to this advice again and again, relearning the lesson that my wellness—and each villager's wellness—is critical to the health of the village as a whole.

When it came to financial backing, again my community stepped up, mostly without my asking. I'd saved enough money that I didn't need to apply for a business loan, but I was far from flush and needed additional funds for marketing assets such as signage, social media branding, and promotions. By this point my supporters could see I was serious and industrious, and they trusted me with their pocket-books. The coffeehouse speakers series (described in the introduction) had been a hit, and people were motivated by my passion and confidence for this bigger vision. My progress and excitement were contagious—the community started to believe in the vision, too, and wanted to be a part of something hopeful and healthy for themselves. They encouraged me to start a GoFundMe campaign so others could donate to my first market, though I quickly shut it down when I realized it had reached $3,000, which was more than enough. Every step forward confirmed to me that this communal way of building was *it*. Things started falling into place, aligning in ways I couldn't have predicted. I experienced a feeling of purpose, a sense that I was fulfilling a role and a cause that took on a life of its own. It felt like a spiritual download that was very much ancestral. Deep in my being I understood the connection between what I was creating and what had been built by those who came before me.

The support kept coming. My inaugural team members donated their time and talents to make sure I had the operational support, branding assets, photography, and event support to run the market successfully. In true village fashion, this was not just me accepting the gifts of my friends but what I call the Great Barter: I exchanged my gifts for theirs. I referred those who had volunteered for me to other events for DJing and photography opportunities.

Perhaps because I didn't know enough to be worried, I was brimming only with optimism and excitement, soaking up the newness of everything. There was no fear of failure, no impostor syndrome (yet)—only a sense of adventure and a deep-seated certainty that I was creating something wonderful and essential for my community. With my community serving as my foundation and my focus, it all came together in just a few months. I did not become gridlocked by ideation or perfectionism. As I envisioned and connected with people, I built. I kept a little notepad with me to chart my steps (this would turn into my first operations manual). I hadn't followed a specific formula or a traditional process for building a business, which I believe would have taken months longer. I simply brought people together who believed in lifting up Black entrepreneurs in the community and used the knowledge and connections we all already had in our possession to move forward. The village was centered from day one, and the power of purpose and alignment propelled it into existence.

The opening night of my first Village Market event in April 2016 was a master class in community. It was a beautiful Friday night, with a breeze and crispness in the air, as if Mother Nature herself were whispering, "Something special is happening." As I stood in the event center, overwhelmed with nerves and happy butterflies in my stomach, considering things I hadn't thought of until that night—Would people have a hard time finding the location? Would entrepreneurs have difficulty unloading their products?—I took in the scene. My dear friends Danyel, GaNene, KJ, Kristen, and Tracey were there, talking through how to manage the front door. Sieje was focused on handling the parking lot. I saw my friend, poet and author Jon Goode, walk in—he would be selling his books that night— and he gave me a big hug. My soul did a somersault with the arrival of each small-business owner. Never did I imagine they wouldn't show up, but I could not contain my excitement when they appeared, and I raced over to hug many of them (I'm a hugger!). The room, overflowing with love, was filled with many familiar faces from the coffee shop and the speaker series, everyone displaying their wares and talents—handmade soaps infused with flowers and herbs, bath creams, wellness cookbooks, plant-based foods, and more.

Just before we opened for customers, I shared with the business owners that this event was different. It was special. I reminded them of what I'd told them in the days leading up to the big night: "You are not just vendors, you are business owners, entrepreneurs, visionaries, and builders." Language matters to a person's mindset, and the term "vendor," I felt, was disposable and generic. As I saw it, the entrepreneurs were the main attraction—the red carpet was for them. These villagers were launching future enterprises and striving to build in excellence and togetherness. I set the standard that we were building differently, that their mindsets had to be counter to the typical self-interested approach. "In the Village Market," I said, "we do not compete against each other; instead, we are complements and supporters of one another. Remember that the success of your neighbor is a reflection of your success. If they need a charger or run out of something, help. Let's collaborate and elevate each other and we will be the best thing for the city of Atlanta." We made a toast to our collective prosperity.

When the doors opened at 7 p.m., I had a big smile on my face—I mean a big 1974 Kool-Aid Man smile—as I watched the space fill with guests. I primed them to embrace the purpose of the Village Market by setting a clear business goal: "Tonight we are going to spend our money within our community; our goal is to circulate thirty thousand dollars among our villagers."

My DJ friend played his mix of soulful house and family-friendly old-school jams to sustain a spirit of positivity. We shopped, ate, and danced—an African dance troupe performed and invited villagers (patrons) to dance with them. It felt like I imagined it would: joyous. Shoppers were excitedly interacting with business owners and sampling wares; people of all ages were enjoying the space; and villagers were supporting one another and proudly spending. We were there to circulate money, after all. I was envisioning each one of these entrepreneurs starting (or furthering) their wealth journey, taking concrete steps together with the community's involvement and benefit. I saw how people genuinely wanted the best for one another. I grabbed my eight-year-old nephew Sean and hugged him tightly. I remember how his eyes looked back at me—they were filled with joy and awe. I silently thanked God for giving me this moment, for giving us all this moment. I felt like we were all stars in the sky who had attracted and circled around one another with our bright lights, creating this beautiful constellation that had become the Village Market. At the end of the event, I was on a high. I heard once that the late artist Prince floated when he walked, actually hovering off the ground. I am confident that, like Prince, I hovered for two days afterward. I will never forget the wonder and beauty of that initial event, how I had an idea and worked with my community to cultivate it and launch it and how I trusted that the community would love and nurture it as if it were their own. I knew that the Village Market was unique, special, and, with so many passionate villagers, that we would all grow it together. And sure enough, we did grow. As we held more markets and profited, I made sure that those who supported me grew as well. I did a dance of joy when I was finally able to actually pay people. I continued to refer my collaborators and entrepreneurs for bigger events and helped them get larger contracts as my social platform grew in the city of Atlanta. After I had a couple of markets under my belt, I secured my first major corporate sponsor thanks to a Black woman who worked at the corporation and who believed in my approach. As the Village Market has grown, it has been nourished by the community and has given back to the community in equal measure. At every step it has been grounded in the fact that the village is the source.

IN THIS COUNTRY, we are fed a continuous stream of inspirational stories about self-made men and women, like culture icons Jay Z,

Rihanna, and Tyler Perry. But the notion that we can or should do it alone is false, for it pushes aside the very thing that enables role models to become role models: the community that supported them. Jay Z was mentored by rapper and record producer Jaz and pooled resources with two other friends to found Roc-A-Fella Records, which produced his first album. Rihanna was signed by Jay Z, who served as a pivotal business mentor to her. Tyler Perry has credited the strong Black women in his family—including his aunt and mother, who nurtured his religious faith—and Oprah as foundational to his life and work. No one is self-made. Not Bill Gates, who founded Microsoft *with* a partner (Paul Allen) and had plenty of business connections and family money. Not Oprah, who, in quoting a Maya Angelou poem, has said, "I come as one, but I stand as ten thousand." When we center a single achiever, we are choosing to erase the people who played a pivotal part in that person's success. Those people who were so integral to the key figure's success become hidden figures, cropped out of the photograph. Buying into this framework of solitary and individual achievement detours us away from the richest source of our gifts: the village. When we rip apart these myths, we are exposed to community, to the real truth of what it takes to build impactfully and meaningfully.

My personal hero, Madam C. J. Walker, widely known as the first Black female "self-made" millionaire in the United States, believed fiercely in the power of the village. Walker made her fortune selling a line of hair-care products for Black women in the late nineteenth century, and she is held up as one of our country's shining rags-to-riches stories. It's understandable why she holds this esteemed spot. Walker was born to enslaved sharecroppers in Louisiana, orphaned at seven, married at fourteen, a mother by fifteen, and widowed by twenty. She worked as a laundress and a cook, went to night school, and built a business empire, all before she was forty. At the time of her death in 1919, she had employed over twenty thousand people (mostly Black women). I drew strength from her perseverance to be successful in the face of so many barriers—racial, gender, economic. In 2020, Netflix produced a stirring series about her called, as it were, *Self-Made*, starring the gifted Octavia Spencer.

But would Walker have described herself as self-made? I honestly believe that the answer is no. She was remarkably successful as an individual, but that wouldn't have been possible without her village. Walker's great-great-granddaughter, Amelia Bundles, wrote a fascinating biography, *On Her Own Ground,* about the critical influence Walker's community had on her success and how she always intended for the village—specifically Black women—to flourish along with her. The popular hair-care products sold by Walker were invented by another enterprising Black woman, Annie Turnbo Malone, a chemist and businesswoman who hired Walker as a sales agent and who became a millionaire herself. Walker's second husband marketed the heck out of her products. Churches and Black civic organizations in her hometowns and all over the South supported her by hosting hair-care demonstrations and purchasing her products (they were amazing products, all told). Walker traveled town to town, salon to salon, church to church, gathering Black women together to train them as saleswomen in their own right, offering them a pathway for financial freedom, which in turn contributed to the prosperity of the company. Many of these saleswomen were able to make in a week what would take them a month to earn as a domestic worker (one of the few professions available to Black women at the time—and an exploitative one at that). When Walker was raising funds to build a factory in Indianapolis to extend the product line, she reached out to other Black pioneers for help. In a letter to entrepreneur and educator Booker T. Washington, whom she hoped would vouch for her in the Black business community, she wrote, "I know I can not do anything alone, so I have decided to make an appeal to the leaders of the race."

Not only did Walker lean on her Black community to expand her business, but she also centered the community at every step. She was able to build her factory and hire Black women in management positions, training them in business operations. At the time, Black women were mainly offered positions as sharecroppers, maids, cooks, and laundresses. They could not vote. They were barred from esteemed professions (such as law and politics), and from enrolling in many universities. So having the opportunity to support themselves and their families and further their training was extraordinary. She funded scholarships for Black students attending Booker T. Washington's Tuskegee Institute (now Tuskegee University) and seed money for Black female entrepreneurs. She contributed generously to Black youth programs, paid off the mortgage of a senior retirement home for formerly enslaved people, and donated to anti-lynching campaigns and World War I relief efforts to improve conditions for Black soldiers.

What drove Walker to reach such economic heights was the betterment and involvement of her community—she lifted as she climbed. Walker's overarching goal was not simply to get rich; it was to empower other Black women to become financially independent and to pay it forward into their communities, which is the foundation for communal and generational wealth. She mentored her team to reinvest in their local schools and churches. She switched from using "I" and "my" in her company's literature to "we" and "our." When she organized a national convention of sales agents in New York City, she made it clear they were not together simply to brainstorm how they could sell more and make more but instead to harness their prosperity for improved living and working conditions for their communities. "I want my agents to feel that their first duty is to humanity," she said, ". . . to do their bit to help advance the best interests of the race." She utilized the social capital that she amassed and encouraged political protest among her agents, organizing them to send President Wilson a telegram decrying race riots, lynchings, and injustices. What Walker was doing was truly groundbreaking: organizing Black female entrepreneurs for political will. Her final words before she passed away were, "I want to live to help my race." Her view of her role, her life assignment (an important concept I unpack in chapter 2), and the impact of her work remained expansive her entire life, going beyond her own household and even her own lifetime. She lived with her community and race in mind, envisioning a better future for all Black people and took concrete steps to improve their chances, financially, educationally, politically, and socially. Her legacy extends beyond basic entrepreneurship; she is a symbol and model for how to build a socially responsible business and how to ingrain collective and generational wealth into the blueprint.

There is no doubt Walker worked hard for her success—doubly hard considering she was laboring in a Jim Crow economy, when both being Black and a woman were considered disqualifying for running a business, let alone for having basic human rights. But she was not self-made. Seeing a person's success through the lens of community does not downgrade their own self-determination and sacrifices or detract from their genius. Walker was a queen operating at her highest level of purpose—her life's calling—with her unique gifts. But she could not have achieved what she did without her community. Together they lifted one another.

Underneath and surrounding the pedestals that our role models stand on is a strong and diverse support system of people who contributed to that person's achievements. When a person has a dream and the determination to go after it, it is powerful to witness the army of builders and supporters who show up to help execute that vision. From the person who provides funding or business mentoring to the friend who listens late at night when hopelessness sets in, these individuals are directly connected to an entrepreneur's forward progress. Not all supporters are loud and in the foreground, but these people are deeply important. Acknowledging the vital power of the supporters doesn't take anything away from the visionary—on the contrary, it reveals how wise a leader is, for they understand the value of relationships and are not afraid to show vulnerability.

It exemplifies leadership. Witnessing a visionary's journey through the prism of the village broadens and deepens their impact.

Some of you may be nodding your head in solidarity. But there may be some for whom this shift in thinking feels uncomfortable. In our society, being anything less than "self-made" is viewed as a blemish on the face of a person's success. This fear of accepting help, or even admitting that you had help, can be especially problematic for those who are pressured by culture, and even by people in their circles, to prove they can do it alone, that they didn't accept "handouts." In general, people do not want to give the impression that their success was given to them, and it's important that their fortitude is seen and worn as a badge of honor. Being able to succeed without the help of an inheritance or even a bank loan can be a point of pride, because success feels more special when it is earned through struggle rather than the support of a village. I understand why it's appealing to feel as if you have done it on your own and why it's exciting to believe that self-made titans exist. It sounds sexy and plays into our desire to prove ourselves against all odds.

But it's so critical to understand the difference between "self-determined" and "self-made." Self-determination is the intrinsic motivation—meaning it comes naturally from within—to continue to press forward. It's your internal bar for excellence, and it is often a requirement of meeting your goals. Self-determination is a deeply held belief that you have a Purpose with a capital *P* (I discuss the importance of identifying purpose in chapter 2), that you have what it takes to seize each opportunity and use it as a stepping stone on your path toward success. Walker certainly had self-determination. Sojourner Truth had it. Mary Ellen Pleasant, a nineteenth-century Black businesswoman and investor who helped fund the Underground Railroad with her fortune, had it. Sheila Johnson, the cofounder of BET, has it. Vegan chef and well-being guru Tabitha Brown has it. Richelieu Dennis, founder of Sundial Brands, has it. Nationally recognized entrepreneur, philanthropist, and Atlanta icon

Herman J. Russell has it. Real estate developer Donahue "Don" Peebles has it. You get the idea.

The reality is that no matter how self-determined a person is, nothing is built in isolation. In fact, we are not wired to build anything on our own. Our brains, according to the latest neuroscience, house neural networks built specifically for socializing and connecting, areas devoted to decoding other people's emotions and behaviors, neurons whose job it is to mirror others' movements and expressions. When I learned this, my first thought was, "Of course nature has gifted us with a road map for how to live: with and for each other, not disconnected and autonomous." We also see this collectivism play out in nature. I recently learned of a cool concept in the scientific world called emergence, which describes, for example, groups of animals, such as a school of fish, an army of ants, or a flock of birds, that work collectively to accomplish something together (hunting, building, protection) that could not be accomplished alone. Humans have this potential, too, a sort of unity consciousness and cooperation that enable us to create together what could never be achieved on our own.

Not only is it unnatural to think we are islands, but it is also harmful to believe that pulling yourself up by your bootstraps is the way forward or that it's even possible. Today, the saying "pull yourself up by your bootstraps" refers to lifting yourself up without help from anyone else, but it originated in the 1800s with a different meaning: to do something so physically impossible that it's absurd. Today's usage, of course, is equally absurd. When we place the full responsibility of success solely on one's own efforts, we fail to acknowledge the role that external elements play, including equal access to education, investment capital, health care, paid time off—all the things that nourish and support a person to operate at their best. The playing field is far from even. White families' net worth—their wealth in terms of assets such as real estate, income, and investments minus debt—is nearly ten times greater than a Black family's net worth. White people aren't ten times more hardworking than

Black people, but they are ten times more advantaged, facing fewer barriers to their upward mobility.

I get how a communal approach may feel counterintuitive to some of you, especially if you are striving to keep your own business afloat. Having to think through a collaborative business strategy can feel like an additional burden. And if you have been let down by others in the past, you may feel wary of depending on anyone else. I have been there too. It's natural to worry that collaborating with others is too complicated or that partnering up may lessen your influence and deplete your resources, placing you in a more vulnerable position. These are all challenges that can crop up in any business (and which I address in chapter 5). But when you are in a like-minded village, the challenges are surmountable and even preventable. The financial risk lessens because you are not funding and resourcing everything alone. The beauty of building with others is that if things start to fall apart—logistically, economically, emotionally—there are people surrounding you who can raise the company and you back up. It is actually *easier* to build with a village outlook. Without community, everything is harder—unnecessarily so. In a self-made paradigm, all resources will be limited, for there is only so much any person can accomplish on their own. Had Madam Walker built her business without community, it would not have taken off as it did.

Another harmful trap of extolling the merits of self-made: It tends to justify success by any means necessary, including stepping on others to get to the top. It's you against the world, a competition, a scarcity and survival mindset where there is only so much to go around and you have to get yours before someone else does; as a result, you may feel warranted in prioritizing your needs above everyone else's, even when that comes at the expense of others. If this is your mindset, I understand how you got here. We've been in a rigged system where only a small percentage receive resources like grants and loans, and it seems that good things continuously happen only to a select few. It makes it hard to want to share the resources that took years to build for fear that you will be giving away what you worked for, that it might send you to the back of the line, where you had to fight just to exist. But this mindset will keep us fighting for scraps and perpetually at the bottom.

I'm not suggesting you shouldn't look out for yourself—you always need to keep your goals and dreams and purpose in mind. Nor am I suggesting you sacrifice everything to the group. The individual is important in a village, and there is plenty of space for the self. But. I am asking you to shift your mindset and recognize that the system is inherently imbalanced and works well only for those with systemic privileges. If we continue to fight among ourselves for scraps, we will never experience more as a collective. We have a saying in the Village Market: "There's enough for all of us." To successfully fight the system, we have to consciously not succumb to it. We must be intentional with how we build. When we shift from an individualistic to a community-centric approach, we are more resilient in the face of challenges, financial hardships, and economic downturns. I recall several instances during the pandemic when the community rallied together to ensure local bookstores and restaurants did not close. People raised money to keep mom-and-pop stores open and purposefully shopped locally to support the businesses in their communities. Because the owners were enmeshed with the community, they did not have to face alone one of the toughest economic crises of our generation. We also become our best selves in community. When we are with others, the energy of connection pushes us to evolve, allowing us to have and experience more. Community sharpens our talents. It helps expand the way we think and deepens our sense of purpose.

When you look at wealth creation in the United States by ethnicity and race, Black folks sit at the bottom. If we are dead last using a design and a mentality that is not working for our people, what is the purpose in continuing to labor in this way? One more Black entrepreneur who is following the "self-made" blueprint to achieve millionaire status is not going to fuel the kind of change and community empowerment needed to close the racial wealth gap. When I attend Black business conferences and hear the crowd go wild when the presenter shouts, "In ten years we are going to create ten thousand Black millionaires!" I am left with the question, But what is the charge for these newly minted millionaires? Is it for them to have a positive social impact or simply to tout the millionaire status? If the only goal is to create more high-net-worth individuals concerned solely with amassing personal wealth, we cannot progress. In recent years, we have seen a surge in Black millionaires, and yet the wealth gap has actually widened. Individual wealth does not translate into community wealth unless it is intentionally and systemically designed to do so. Today, the median wealth for Black households is just $24,000, compared to a median wealth of $134,000 for white households. If the downward trend for Black people continues, we are on track to zero median wealth by 2053, according to the Institute for Policy Studies. We need visionaries and builders who are building differently, more inclusively. We need leaders who center the community with every step.

The notions of individualism and being self-made pull us away from the surest, safest, and most prosperous way for everyone to thrive. Madam C. J. Walker provides us with only one example of how a village mindset can lead to prosperity for Black communities. Perhaps the most shining illustration in this country was the Greenwood District of Tulsa, Oklahoma, designated as the first Black Wall Street and also, horrifically, the setting of the Tulsa Race Massacre. I first learned about Black Wall Street when I was an undergraduate in college. In 1905, at a time when Black people were not allowed to live in white neighborhoods, O. W. Gurley, a Black entrepreneur, purchased forty acres of land in Tulsa, which he then divided and sold only to Black people. By 1921, these forty acres had become a flourishing community of nine thousand people, a town filled with homes, stores, schools, beauty parlors, and churches.

(Churches—the nucleus for many a civil rights movement—were villages in and of themselves, providing a safe place to rest, to be fed, and to be educated.) Tragically, Black Wall Street was burned to the ground in a single night by an angry white mob. The Tulsa Race Massacre cost three hundred people (mostly Black) their lives; many more were injured, and livelihoods were lost. Insurance companies refused to honor any claims; as a result, surviving proprietors had nothing to rebuild with. Learning of this event was both inspiring and heartbreaking for me—inspiring because I hadn't heard many stories of Black resiliency and Black empires at that point in my life; heartbreaking because it underscored the awful fact that wherever there is Black progress, there is protest, often violent, against it.

Black Wall Street is not an anomaly. There are dozens of Black Wall Streets in our country's history, examples of Black entrepreneurs banding together to prosper only to be held back or have their businesses abolished by systemic or targeted racism. In Richmond, Virginia, the Jackson Ward District flourished in the late 1800s, with banks (one headed by Maggie Lena Walker, the first Black woman to run a bank), insurance companies, and theaters. That thriving community fell victim to 1950s racist practices, such as redlining, redistricting, and white flight, cutting off the area physically and financially. Mound Bayou, Mississippi, founded as an all-Black town for formerly enslaved people in 1887, became a profitable center for cotton-industry businesses and birthed an ecosystem of schools, hospitals, newspapers, and banks. Mound Bayou was where politically targeted African Americans sought refuge and where the mother of Emmett Till found safe haven during her son's trial. Today, it is a shadow of its former self—economic opportunities dried up, and many families and young people left for larger towns and cities.

Despite the destruction of physical representations of dozens of Black Wall Streets, their legacy of group economics (a business strategy I explore in chapter 7) and the strength of the beloved community inspires today's village-made icons. Robert Smith, the wealthiest Black man in America, traces part of his generational tree to Tulsa's Greenwood District. Smith credits his Tulsa roots and understanding of the "blanket of care" of community with helping to form his business values. Smith became the first Black man to sign the Giving Pledge, vowing to contribute the majority of his wealth to philanthropic causes.

One reason it is so critical for successful Black entrepreneurs like Smith to acknowledge the village that grew them—and to attest that they operate in community—is because it helps deconstruct the stereotype that "if they can do it all by themselves, anyone can do it." If it were so easily achievable to pull yourself up by your bootstraps and prosper, we wouldn't look only to Robert Smith and Oprah, who have donated millions to education and Black cultural causes, as symbols of success. We'd have so many examples that we would no longer have to hold these people up as the exceptions. Not only that, but we would also have many more wealthy Black individuals positioned to give back to their villages, so we'd see many communities thriving, not just one Black individual here or there showing up on a list of "the country's wealthiest."

We see the same communal spirit our ancestors possessed in present-day entrepreneurial icons like Issa Rae and Richelieu Dennis. Rae's umbrella company, Hoorae, houses a village of media companies to incubate and support Black media creators. She recently became a co-owner of Hilltop Coffee & Kitchen in Los Angeles, where she grew up, to introduce community-centered, Black-owned businesses into the city. Dennis made his fortune making and selling the Sundial Brands' shea butter beauty line (inspired by his Liberian grandmother's homemade soaps and lotions) through what he calls "community commerce"—giving underserved communities the tools and opportunities to find entrepreneurial success, value that gets invested back into the community. In 2013, Dennis's Sundial Brands acquired Madam C. J. Walker's product lines, marking a significant milestone thirty-two years after Walker's heirs initially sold the company. Following the acquisition, Sundial Brands successfully launched the distribution of these products at Sephora. Through the sale of his company to Unilever, Dennis launched the New Voices Fund, a nonprofit that invests in and empowers female Black entrepreneurs and has kept the legacy of Madam C. J. Walker alive. The fund has invested in several leading brands, such as Slutty Vegan and the Lip Bar. The financial backing catapulted these founders' success and growth. The fund also supported the Black women–owned companies the Honey Pot and Mielle Organics in reaching an estimate of eight- and nine-figure acquisition deals. Dennis took the baton that was passed to him and is forging a new generation of Black wealth and preserving the legacy of those who came before him. I often marvel at the intergenerational evolution set in motion by a young laundress a century ago, who found her purpose as an entrepreneur and community leader, and how the seeds she sowed continue to bear fruit for generations. It is with this same vision of far-reaching community prosperity that I plant my seeds with my village, with the hope and intention that the impact continues to lift my family and my people long after I am gone.

We can do powerful and transformative things together, especially when we are well, supported, and intentional, when we are following our soul's calling and using our unique gifts to lift up others. I loved learning about the Black Panthers' Free Breakfast for School Children Program that launched at a single church in the late 1960s in Oakland and expanded to forty-five sites across the country. Relying on donations from local food pantries and grocery stores—and volunteer hours from home cooks—the program fed nutritious breakfasts to thousands of children who would have otherwise gone hungry—and test scores skyrocketed. The program is credited with pioneering the free breakfast programs offered today in public schools. My heart swelled when I read about the Freedom House Ambulance Service, the first paramedic service in the country, comprised of twenty-five Black men. The ambulance service launched

in 1967 in Pittsburgh's Hill District, a partnership between an ambulance driver and CEO, a social worker, and the doctor who helped
invent CPR.

For me, the community has been a safe place to dream, grow,
and find alignment with others whose purposes match up with
mine. Along with my friends, I've been able to actualize a life and
livelihood that's worthwhile. In my vulnerable moments, when I was
worried about the state of my nonprofit and it seemed like everything was falling apart, I clung to my village and they helped me put
it back together again. My community has provided me a safety net
and together we've been able to be our best and highest selves.

I have experienced this collective spirit during volunteer work
after massive tornadoes wreaked havoc in Alabama, when my grandfather's house was decimated by a storm, when floodwaters rose
across the Bahamas, and during the water crisis in Jackson, Mississippi. People hold on to one another, and for a moment in a time of
crisis, the world stands still—race, gender, religion, and sexual orien-
tation do not matter and we simply see the humanity in one another.
The day after Katrina slammed into the Gulf Coast as a category 5
hurricane, I remember news circulating in our community about the
catastrophic devastation it had unleashed on New Orleans and the
Gulf Coast. My best friend's family lives on the Gulf Coast, and during our daily talks she shared appalling stories of worsening conditions. Seeking refuge from the storm, coastal residents from Gulf
states had traveled inland, driving for hours and relying on strangers
for food, water, gas, and shelter—these things were in short supply,
but goodwill was not. As people processed the next steps, everyday
folk, community-based organizations, faith-based organizations, and
other neighborhood groups strategized how to support recovery efforts. People volunteered at food banks, joined cleanup crews, and
donated baby formula, clothing, and bedding. Support came from
both local individuals and governments as far away as Kuwait and
Singapore. The sports community galvanized resources, and tech

companies set up donation pages. The larger community was focused on one mission: to help as many people as they could.

I believe tragedies often remind us that at our core we are innately united—we are love, flawed and often muddied by life but connected and meant to exist and overcome together. We show up beautifully when we are all pitching in, fulfilling necessary purposes and roles, using our gifts and networks and resources for the betterment of everyone in the village.

But we should not just show up in times of tragedy. We should strive for this level of unity all the time. If we contribute the same effort, love, and intention in all spaces of communal purpose, including building businesses and pursuing vocations, just imagine how much we can accomplish! It should not take a Hurricane Katrina to bring us together with a single-minded purpose. We know what we are capable of in the darkest of hours; now we must bring that same collective energy and sense of purpose to our enterprises and the everyday. To fully tap into the powerful energy source of the village consistently and believably and to build lives of prosperity for ourselves and future generations—to build collective generational wealth—we must recalibrate and shift our mindset. We must leave the myth of self-made behind and recognize that collective prosperity is within our reach and that equity, joy, and purpose lies in our togetherness.

# TWO

# Discovering Your Purpose and Getting into Alignment

FOR CAREER DAY IN THIRD GRADE, I STOOD IN FRONT OF MY class, dressed in a sweater and plum corduroy trousers (like my teacher Mrs. Drake), and proudly told everyone, with a slight stutter, "When I grow up, I am going to be a teacher." My father wanted me to be a doctor or a dentist, like his cousin Delois, the first and only dentist in the family. But my teachers were beacons of light for me, and I wanted to be just like them. While my parents appreciated teachers, my father felt that doctors and dentists had greater financial security, which meant a life of safety and opportunities for me. Now, I was a devout daddy's girl, but I was determined. "No," I told him. "I'm going to be a teacher."

After college, I began teaching high school English at Madison Shannon Palmer in Marks, Mississippi. I loved my cozy classroom, where I draped the walls with quotes from African American writers.

I adored my old-school chalkboard and green record book, where I marked students' attendance and grades. (Eventually, the school upgraded to whiteboards and digital recordkeeping, which I begrudgingly accepted.) But most of all I loved my students, my little village that I was nurturing within those four walls. I greeted my high schoolers when they walked through the door with a high five, a "dap" (fist bump), a hug, or a giant smile, reassuring them that when they entered the classroom, they were safe, loved, and seen. Little third-grade Lakeysha would have been thrilled to see me, as an adult, diving into deep discussions of classic books with students or instructing them on "bell ringer activities" (assignments students could start as they rolled into the room). Whether it was a selection of blues music (we were in the Mississippi Delta, after all, the birthplace of the blues) or a piece of art created by an African American they were asked to write about, I found ways to introduce inspiring Black luminaries to validate my students' perspectives while teaching the fundamentals of English literature. Teaching was more than just a profession to me. It filled me with purpose.

Purpose is a calling that is sacred to you but also bigger than you. It's often defined as the reason for which something is done or created or for which something exists. I think of purpose like being in a healthy relationship: It is and feels like love; it transforms you and fills you up. It's consistent, but it challenges you to evolve and expand the way that you think and opens you to new perspectives. Purpose nourishes you and grants you peace. For me, it is a tight embrace that lingers, a home and a place of refuge for my light, my ideas, my gifts. Professionally, and as I've journeyed as an entrepreneur, purpose has led me to discover and attract more of my people. It has given me clarity and fuel to fulfill my mission.

This is how I felt for four years at Palmer. I aimed to help my students dream that more was possible for them beyond the gravel roads and cotton fields. I exposed them to writers with humble beginnings, authors like Dr. Maya Angelou, who was from Stamps,

Arkansas, and raised by her grandmother. Her upbringing resembled that of many of my students—a good number of them were also raised by their grandmothers. I often asked them: "Is there a future Dr. Maya Angelou in this class? Who in the class will bring light to Quitman County?" As I fed their minds, I watched as they expanded their belief in what was possible for them. When they graduated from high school and became the first to go to college, I helped them set up and decorate their dorm rooms. I proudly sat in the audience as former students defended their dissertations for their doctorate degrees. All this was purpose work—my life was intrinsically tied to my students and theirs to mine. Year after year, I evolved as my purpose continued to unfold. I believe that purpose is revealed as you get to know yourself, your talents, and your value to the world. When you begin to feel and follow your purpose, there's a flow to your life. You are motivated and inspired by what you are building and who you are building with. People who are like-minded seem to appear in your life at the right moments and give you determination to keep pursuing the vision you see in your mind. Purpose puts a clear path before you and you feel unstoppable. You see the return on your investment of time, you see results, and you feel accomplished. You sense that you are where you are meant to be, doing what you are meant to do.

In my fifth year at Palmer, however, I sensed the sun would be setting on my time there. The environment had changed for me— with some discord developing among the staff (I share more about this challenging time in chapter 5)—and I began to feel out of place and isolated. The fullness I experienced in my early years slowly emptied out. While I still loved teaching my students, the lack of camaraderie and support affected me deeply. My soul was no longer at home there. I still felt that my purpose was to teach, just not at Palmer.

So when an opportunity to teach English at Callaway High School in the capital city of Jackson came up, I excitedly took it. I was familiar with Jackson, as I'd lived there for four years while attending Tougaloo College. Though I was nervous to leave Palmer,

I viewed it as a great opportunity to stretch myself and grow. Ultimately I wanted to live in Atlanta, but I saw Callaway as a beautiful stop on my journey, and it just felt like the right next move.

I think of these new chapters as life assignments, and I believe that when we are fulfilling our assignments—when we are saying yes to the new opportunities that cross our paths—there's a feeling of alignment, as if it is being orchestrated for our greater good. Some may call it fate; others, serendipity. I see this beautiful alignment, when you stop chasing things and you begin to attract them, as divine. When I am in divine alignment, it seems that things begin to work effortlessly. I draw in my people, my village. I do not have to overstate my value or perform or convince, which can leave me feeling sales-y. When you are in alignment, people *see* you and are excited about your ideas and talents. I met my literary agent, Rebecca, because she heard me talking about the village on my friend's podcast and *saw* my potential. We started the journey of writing this book soon after. Though I hadn't written a book before, I'd always dreamed of becoming a writer. I knew little about the formal publishing process, but she assured me that she'd have my back. The experience was alignment on steroids, and my passion for the village attracted Rebecca to my story. Even if you have some fear of the unknown, when things are aligning for you, there is also a sense of excitement and peace for what's ahead. When you are in alignment, you begin to see where the pieces fit in the puzzle and you recognize and identify the people who can help you put the puzzle together.

While I expected to be tested at Callaway, I was taken aback by the challenges—a city environment, a new culture, and kids who weren't afraid to test me and see what I was really about. I had to revamp my approach to connect with my new students. They were very bright, like my students at Palmer, but they were also different— vocal and assertive. Respect was not a given; it had to be earned. I tuned in to the things that grabbed their attention, like their love of arguing with one another. I tapped in and told them that they could no longer argue without structure—they had to debate. "Debate?" they scoffed. "Yes," I told them, and then played the 2007 movie *The Great Debaters*. They were captivated. I divided my classroom in two groups and taught them the rules and art of debate. We debated Shakespeare's play *Othello* and the pros and cons of President Obama's first six months in office. They had an opportunity to take ownership of their learning, choosing what poems and short stories we'd examine. After a couple of weeks, we found our cadence and our flow as a class. I'd gained their respect.

Next door to my classroom was a special education classroom, and I started to nurture a relationship with one of the teachers, a jazzy, vibrant woman in her early fifties named Mrs. Frances Etheridge. She was a glowing light with a big personality, naturally funny, and we connected more as the year went on, playing tennis after school some days. (She beat me every match.) One day, Mrs. E., as I'd started to call her, asked if I wouldn't mind volunteering some time to assist some of her students—she saw something in me that told her I could work with all levels of students. I said yes because of how much I adored and respected her, and a few times each month I helped various students with writing and reading. After observing me with her students, she encouraged me to take the special education exam. I was content in my current role and felt that my strength was in teaching honors and AP English, so I said no. But the suggestion stuck in my head, especially since Mrs. E. was one of the people at school who believed in my work and potential. So once she planted the seed, it was rooted. Even though it was not my vision for myself, I decided to take the exam. Blame it on being in my twenties, but I almost overslept and missed it—I didn't even study for it and had no idea if I would pass or not. I wasn't bothered by it either way and went on with my life.

By this point, I'd been at Callaway for eleven months and I'd started interviewing for teaching positions in Atlanta. The magic I'd experienced years earlier at the Black Arts Festival—being steeped in a Black communal experience that was so dynamic and welcoming—was still with me, and subsequent visits to the city had confirmed that Atlanta was where I wanted to be. My mother, who was insistent that I spread my wings and fly to where I could further blossom, had given me her blessing to move. A couple years prior, she'd been diagnosed with lupus, and I didn't want to leave her. I was part of her support system, and most of my weekends I was back in Batesville with her, my little sister, Whitney, my brother, Roderick, and my dad. But when she learned of my interest in Atlanta, she practically pushed me out of the nest and demanded that I fly again. After she visited Atlanta on a trip with me, she became certain it was where I needed to be, where I could evolve and blossom even more into the special person she saw when she looked at me. I did not always know how to receive her nudging—I wasn't sure if she was pushing me away or pushing me to grow. (I've since learned that she saw something in me that I couldn't yet see for myself and was pushing me so that I could grow.) So I began to apply for jobs, including an English teacher position at South Cobb High School, a magnet school in the greater Atlanta metro area. When I returned home to Jackson, the principal from South Cobb, Dr. Hosey, called to say they had been so impressed with me but that a teacher with more seniority wanted to transfer, and so the job was filled. I was crushed. But just before he hung up, he said, "Now, if you had a special education certification, I could offer you a special education job." I couldn't believe it! A week earlier I'd received the results of my special education certification in the mail—I'd passed. I could not wait to share the news with Mrs. E. Without her encouragement, I would not have taken the exam.

When you are in alignment, a domino effect happens: the pieces begin to fall, guiding you toward your purpose and assignments that place you in your life's flow. But you must say yes to the assignments that cross your path without expecting anything in return. Saying yes to Mrs. E., to the invitation of the assignment—working with her students and then taking the exam—was divine alignment for me. It required me to say yes, even though I did not know what was on the other side. I simply wanted to use my gifts to serve something higher than myself, to help Mrs. E.'s students. When you are in alignment, you are prompted to take direction from others who mean you well and who are living purposefully. Alignment also places you in a safer environment where you can trust yourself and the people around you. Alignment is inherently communal, because a person's evolution is reliant on connecting and working with others; it's a state and mindset that is so different from the "self-made" construct, where any progress is supposedly up to you and you alone.

At South Cobb, I evolved in ways that tipped over more dominoes along my path. I was walking down the hallway one day, contemplating how to get more involved with the tennis community, when the athletic director, a fast-talking man, stopped me and said, "I heard you've got experience writing grants." I told him yes, I had done a little grant writing. "Well, I'd love to put you on a project with a couple of teachers who are trying to get us a big grant for an after-school program." I didn't think twice about my response—I said yes. Even though I had a full class load and was a new kid on the block, I was committed to this school and to growing my relationship with this community in whatever way I could. Our mighty team of three worked hard at writing that grant. When we submitted the proposal, we had no expectation of what might happen; all we knew is that we'd given it everything we could have.

A few months later, we received the incredible news that we had won the grant! The after-school program we'd envisioned, Fly Zone, could launch. We hired a program director and got the program off the ground, with me as the assistant director. The kids loved it. But within a few months, the director had to leave. Dr. Hosey called me into his office and offered me the position. It wasn't something I ever saw myself doing. But I was so moved that he saw the potential in me that—again—I said yes. (Apparently, I was having a Shonda Rhimes moment and it was my Year of Yes.) And I'm so glad I did. I led the program for a year, on top of teaching and coaching basketball. We had so much success that my supervisor asked me to apply for a position at GADOE to work with after-school programs around the state. That's what's so beautiful about the subtle and unexpected ways alignment happens. When you say yes to assignments, when you give your all when your community needs you, you fall into alignment and you grow. One day you are walking down the hallway thinking about your tennis game, and the next day you are leading training sessions across the state of Georgia to improve the lives of the next generation. I showed up fully in each moment of opportunity, without an expectation that what I was working on would necessarily flow back to me. Alignment is a beautiful rhythm, a harmonious relationship among action, intention, and purpose. You feel confident in the work that you're doing, and it feels true to your values.

This feeling of harmony is how I knew I was fulfilling my assignment during my years of teaching my students and training teachers. The opportunities kept coming, and I trusted enough in these happenings—and in the people offering them—to say yes. I was affirmed at every step. I was fully in alignment.

And yet.

In 2018, after having spent six years at GADOE, something had decidedly shifted. I was feeling drawn to pour my all into the Village Market, which I'd been building since 2016. My "side" passion project seeped into every free moment I had during the day and consumed my early mornings and late nights. I began to envision my life outside of education. But I was afraid. I'd never been a full-time business owner. I'd never even taken a business class. Still, I knew how to bring people together and galvanize them around a shared mission. And that mission—though it had been fulfilled for a long time as a teacher—was beginning to take new shape. I thought about that work—about creating a beloved community for the Black entrepreneurs around me—when I woke up in the morning and before I went to sleep at night.

We can have more than one purpose, and the gifts and skills we hone along one purposeful pathway can be used to chart other routes, to shape other creations. If we trust our heart's stirrings and answer the needs of our community, new purposes can be revealed to us. However, this transition can feel disorienting. While I was falling deeply in love with the Village Market, I felt unsettled and off my center. I was experiencing a sort of misalignment in my role with GADOE. I can tell you many things that were problematic with the position and its leadership, but the biggest thing that was off was *me*. The more time I spent building out my Village Market dream, the more I was finding it difficult to be in a relationship with my role at GADOE. I began to struggle with some of my coworkers and my manager. The things that used to feel easy—attending extra meetings, agreeing to projects that weren't strictly in my job description, and just generally taking on more—now felt hard. I was more agitated than usual, which my friends will tell you is not who I am. I had lost the joy and zeal I normally had. More and more, I accepted that I'd finished my assignment at GADOE and overstayed my time. My journey was complete.

When you're out of alignment, things aren't smooth. Most interactions feel forced and depleting. You go about life like a Ferris wheel, slowly in a circle, arriving at the same destination. For some, this may feel like a grave detachment (which I talk about more in chapter 6). When we are out of alignment, it takes from us—from our energy, our spirit, our creativity—and never pours back into us. It steals passion and erodes our belief in ourselves. Our inner knowing is telling us that we are meant for more than this state of unease, but we feel stuck and lost. The things that normally make us come alive—work trips, special projects, connecting with coworkers—don't do it for us anymore. We all have down moments—even when we're in alignment!—but when lackluster moments accumulate, they can turn into lackluster days and then weeks, creating a state of lethargy. When you are in a relationship that is long overdue to end, but you stay—be it a professional relationship, romantic, or with a friend—the relationship brings out the worst in you and gnaws at your self-esteem and peace.

This was where I found myself, stretched too thin and unable to fully connect to my work anymore. It finally reached a crisis point when I said no to helping a supervisor on a project that was not related to my department or my responsibilities, in part because past experience had taught me that I'd end up doing all the work but also because I subconsciously knew that refusing her would create a situation that would force me to leave. Predictably, I was officially called out for insubordination. My managers were compelled to say, "Dr. Hallmon, this is not working," and I resolutely agreed. It definitely wasn't working, and that was my last day.

Looking back, I see my heart wasn't in it and I should have left months before. But I was terrified to take the leap away from my identity as an educator into the uncharted waters of entrepreneurship. Education was my passion and what I'd known for my whole professional life; it was also my financial security. But we often stay on a path far too long because our identity is tied to it. It's OK to change your mind, to pivot, and to want something different for yourself. I was evolving. Even so, I still carried some worry about supporting myself as a full-time entrepreneur; in education, there'd been a reliable paycheck, health benefits, a regular schedule, and job security. Entrepreneurship meant giving up all of that. But I had saved enough money for several months of a financial cushion—I needed a soft landing in order to take a leap of faith. That's what faith is, when you have nothing else to rely on but your gut sense and God. It's one of the hardest things to do in life. But moving forward with faith—and with community—changes lives and changes you.

While making the final drive to the office to turn in my things, I decided to check my work voicemail one last time. I tapped the button wistfully, aware of the finality. We don't always experience one emotion all by itself, especially when we're in the midst of major transitions. I was feeling some relief but also a sense of bewilderment at what I was about to take on. Now, I've come to understand that big feelings that go in all directions are not necessarily signs of misalignment but rather the natural consequence of moving through a liminal space, times when we are in transit from one place or role to another. But at the time, the mix of emotions was scary. Was I making the right choice by following my passion? I still had the faith, but, as I waited for my voicemail to play, I also recognized that I was *scared*.

I will never forget listening to the message as I made the turn near the old Atlanta Braves stadium. A woman from the Atlanta Public Schools (APS) system who had attended one of my professional development trainings asked that I contact her about a contract opportunity. I called her first thing on Monday. "Dr. Hallmon! We need a facilitator for a professional development training coming up, and my colleagues and I were in your session over the summer. We want to hire you if you can take outside work." The timing could not have been more perfect. "It just so happens," I told her, "that as of last Friday I no longer work at GADOE and now I *can* take outside work." So for the next three months, I did a one-day monthly training for APS, which paid the equivalent of my entire monthly salary at GADOE.

It was a moment that illuminated for me just how much could happen outside of GADOE—and how the universe took care of me, even when I was afraid. That I had that much security and protection, even in the face of uncertainty, moved me to tears. It was a potent reminder that the domino effect of alignment doesn't always reveal itself right away. I had done this training back in the summer, without a paycheck attached to it, simply because I loved doing it. Months later, this person had shown up in my life when I needed her to. The last day I worked as a traditional educator was the first day I became a paid speaker. It also reinforced for me the idea that assignments and alignment and purpose are action oriented—they require doing. And doing requires taking risks.

When I honored that calling to run the Village Market full-time, my spirit felt settled. It seemed as though my soul exhaled. I heard the whisper of purpose affirming me that I was doing the work I was sent here to do. I moved back into alignment. And although I had left education as a career, the gifts and skills that were so fundamental to my teaching—relationship building, knowledge sharing, empathy, a reverence for learning, a need to nurture—were not lost. They were re*purposed* in my new community, into the Village Market.

Were there days that I was uncertain? Absolutely. Working in your purpose does not mean there won't be challenges. I think about the day I drove back to school for the last time, how unsure I was about what would come next. But doubt and alignment can coexist. Some days, purpose and panic may go hand in hand, and that's OK, because the resolute knowledge that you are serving a greater good will get you through the trying times. And so will a loving community. They will have your back. For you cannot and should not do anything all by yourself.

WE ARE, EACH one of us, sitting on this earth tasked with *assignments,* small but important actions that serve ourselves and others, and our assignments unfurl into *alignment,* a forward momentum where everything falls into place. This alignment is linked to our greater *purpose,* that big-picture calling, which is tethered to other people. The three work in tandem. Assignments—the opportunities we say yes to because they spark something in us or happen to arrive just when we need them—put us in a position to have our purpose or purposes, plural, revealed to us. As we journey through life's seasons, assignments give us direction and meaning and place us on a path forward. I cannot express enough that life assignments require *doing.* It requires you to show up for Zoom meetings and community events, to respond to emails, to volunteer when you can. When you show up, I believe it tells the universe that you have reverence for the work, for relationships, that you can be trusted with the next thing.

Even if you hit a roadblock, purpose gives you intrinsic motivation to find another route. It pushes you beyond self-interest and expands your capacity to serve the community. Putting yourself out there can feel like a professional risk, and it can be frightening, but when we do it with the village, it becomes less scary because you are not doing so alone.

Purpose signifies many different things to different people. Michael Bernard Beckwith, a powerful spiritual teacher and minister whom I've learned a great deal from, talks about purpose as a spiritual destiny that each of us possesses, a destiny we fulfill when we answer the essential questions: What is the universe's idea of my life? What do I already have to serve that vision? What do I have to let go of in order to step into my assignments and purpose? Purpose involves an evolution of our self and our lives, of our career goals, and of the community we are engaged with. This evolution often requires that we shed certain preconceptions—limitations or status-quo constructs handed to us by society, all the "can'ts" and "shoulds" and "should nots"—in order to open up space for what *can* be. I love the analogy that Beckwith uses to illustrate this shift, that of a little acorn that has to let go of its smallness in order to become the big oak tree.

Purpose is more than just having a goal. Goals—starting a business, hiring your first employee, setting up your website, or owning your first property—are wonderful, but they are concrete things you can accomplish and check off your list. A business that has purpose woven into it is stacked for success, for it becomes something greater than an individual ego or wealth or ticking off a checklist—it is now feeding you on a deep level and flowing into the community you wish to serve, a conduit for the togetherness that will spark growth and prosperity. Opening a grocery store is a goal; opening a store in a food desert to give residents access to healthy, affordable food is a purpose. Starting an insurance business is a goal; offering low-cost insurance to those who cannot afford it is a purpose. As an entrepreneur, discovering and centering your purpose is critical, for it will be your compass as you build your business and your village. Purpose not only uplifts and advances you; its energy also grabs as many people as possible and changes the course of their lives, providing hope, refuge, and belonging.

Social scientists define "purpose" as a stable intention to accomplish something that is meaningful to the self and to the world beyond—and have found that a strong sense of purpose is linked to increased happiness, better health, and longevity. Having meaning in life—an understanding about one's place in the world and the values one holds—can buffer us against the harmful physical and mental effects of trauma and stress, research finds. It gives us hope, a reason to move forward. The Japanese have a word for it: *ikigai*, something to live for, the joy and goal of living. People with *ikigai* actually live longer than those without *ikigai*.

We can look to certain people who beautifully illustrate the law of purpose, visionaries who embraced their village assignments, who were swept into alignment toward their purpose and who transformed many lives in the process. Martin Luther King Jr. clearly fulfilled his assignments, from the time he entered into the ministry as a young man to helping lead the 1955 Montgomery bus boycott (started by two Black women fulfilling their assignments—Claudette Colvin at the age of fifteen and Rosa Parks at the age of forty-two, both of whom refused to give up their seats). King's relentless acceptance of his assignments—some of which involved serving jail time and bodily harm—ignited one of the largest civil rights movements in our nation's history, a communal groundswell that flowed outward from the Deep South to Washington, DC, to Florida, New York, Maine, Illinois, and beyond.

Stacey Abrams found her purpose early on: fighting for the rights of disenfranchised Georgians and galvanizing people to believe change was possible. From becoming the first Black woman named House minority leader in the Georgia legislature (where she expanded Medicaid and focused on criminal justice reform) to founding the nonpartisan organizations New Georgia Project and Fair Fight to counter voter suppression (which is largely credited for securing President Biden's win in 2020), her assignments elevated those in the village who need help the most. But her crowning achievement, I believe, her Purpose with a capital *P*, was to ignite a fire of passion in Georgians, to help them feel that change could happen—even in the embattled South. Though there are many organizations and leaders that made change possible in Georgia, Abrams and her supporters energized the populace into making Georgia a contender in the fight for democracy. I got to know Stacey when she was running for governor of Georgia. We met when she added my Village Market event as a stop during her campaign run. Afterward, she became a text away, always eager to support the work of the Village. What I didn't realize until later was how talented she was at entrepreneurship, how she was able to build businesses around purpose, to scale enterprises that had deep social impact and challenged systems. Among several ventures, she cofounded Nourish, a beverage company for infants and toddlers, and later pivoted the business to Now, a no-hassle invoicing system for small businesses. As a serial entrepreneur with a social justice focus, she became a role model for me in that space as well.

President Barack Obama is another brilliant example of someone whose trajectory of assignments spiraled up and pulled people into his purpose. Obama started out fulfilling hyperlocalized but important assignments: He was a community organizer on Chicago's South Side, he set up job training and tutoring for college-bound residents, and he organized Illinois voter registration campaigns. Who knew his alignment would culminate in a nationwide movement of change and in giving the United States its first Black president? "Yes, we can!" swept across this country, and millions of people believed that we could experience a better America together. His movement united a diverse group of eager voters to believe in our collective powers. He became a symbol of hope when our country was desperate for a ribbon in the sky.

When President Biden decided not to pursue a second term, Vice President Kamala Harris accepted the call to lead the Democratic ballot. Within hours of the announcement, Win With Black Women raised $1.6 million to support the campaign. Days after, Black, white, and Latino people began organizing Zoom calls, raising money, volunteering, and utilizing their social media platforms to engage their followers to join in the mission. There was a surge of collective excitement and a willingness to fight for the country's future and continued civil rights progress. This moment wasn't just centered on VP Harris; it was also about what the people believed her campaign could achieve: freedom, resources, mobility, and, above all, joy. People fueled this mission—it took a collective effort of everyday people coming together in pursuit of something better.

Everyone, including visionaries who fuel societal transformations, grow incrementally. We all start as acorns. Our assignments are delivered and accepted in small doses in the beginning, and it is sustained growth over time that results in the oak tree. I am reminded through individuals in my Atlanta community and the incredible "everyday" people I meet on my travels that there are villagers everywhere who are accepting their assignments and living and working in their purpose, carrying on the important collective work of our ancestors, even if they're not starting national movements.

Purpose is just as powerful when it's intentionally local and seeped into our small businesses. Every start-up that is community focused helps drive us to create generational change and wealth. My friend Angel Gregorio is one of those village visionaries who started locally (though she has a national reach). Angel is changing lives by providing much-needed opportunities for Black female businesses in the service industry to occupy commercial space in DC, one of the most expensive commercial real estate markets in the country. On a whim in 2016, she launched her first venture in DC, Spice Suite, when she walked by an empty retail space and felt moved to own a spice shop (assignment pivot—she was an assistant principal at the time!). She then opened it up to Black female entrepreneurs who needed free pop-up space to sell their products (assignment!). It did so well (alignment!) that she expanded into a new location with Black and Forth, a 7,500-square-foot commercial mall space for Black female–owned beauty businesses. On the weekends, she hosts a farmers' market featuring Black farmers, providing an opportunity for them to sell their produce. Angel also employs formerly incarcerated people, in part because she has family members who have been imprisoned—she understands firsthand the employment challenges they face and how they need a community of support. Her purpose—economic empowerment for Black women—continues to provide gifts to her community in ways she couldn't have envisioned when she took that fortuitous stroll by the empty storefront. When you are in your purpose, people will benefit greatly from what you are creating. I envision octopus arms reaching out and grabbing opportunities in many directions—and when you're aligned with your purpose, those arms have even more collaborators to grasp on to!

Morgan DeBaun, founder of Blavity and AfroTech—the latter is the largest tech conference in the country for Black millennials—is another person who has fulfilled assignment after assignment and is riding the wave of alignment. Nearly a decade ago, she felt the need to create a safe space where Black people in the tech field could network and expose their gifts to the world. In 2016, she launched AfroTech in San Francisco to do just that, and since then her "little" idea has gone global—she is now partnering with leaders and innovators in many locales to expand the conference. Before AfroTech, there was nothing for Black tech entrepreneurs at scale, who sorely needed support: Less than 2 percent of venture capital money makes its way to Black entrepreneurs (and less than 1 percent for female Black business owners).

Purpose can be revealed in a time of sorrow and need and even joy. It lives within us and when it's time to appear, it does. If it is lying dormant, it will nag at you until you recognize it. When it settles in you, it soothes the parts of you that have been misunderstood, the parts of you that did not always fit; it makes sense of the ideas and visions and moves you to action. It anoints your ideas and draws supportive people to you.

While some of us know our purpose early on, for others it's not so clear. It can be unsettling to be in the process of searching, feeling uncertain about your gifts or passions or path. My sister went through a period like this before joining the Village Retail, my brick-and-mortar store, as the operations manager. Until then, her jobs were good, but they did not feel purposeful. She wrestled with feeling unfulfilled, and I would tell her, "You're feeling unsettled because your life was meant for more." That restlessness was her purpose, nagging her to a place of discomfort because it needed to be activated. "What would you like to do?" I asked. She told me, "I am not sure right now, but I know it's not this." I encouraged her to use this time of not knowing as a gift, as an opportunity for discovery, for soul searching: "What lights up your heart?" I asked her. "What feeling do you want to experience?"

My sister often talks about how fulfilling her life is now—she revels in the joy and pride she feels meeting customers from all over the world and working closely with the entrepreneurs in the Village Retail. Even on challenging and stressful days, she still feels purposeful because she knows those are simply moments—and the good and the tough days are all worth it.

If you are not entirely sure what direction to take your gifts, you may need to do some internal work—more time spent in solitude tuning in to your heart—to get closer to finding your next purpose. Even for those who do not have a spiritual practice, I believe it is essential to spend time in solitude to unplug from distractions—social media and the busyness of life—so we can sit with ourselves and hear what makes us come alive. This may not be easy at first. The thoughts can be rough. But it gets easier with practice. We grow more comfortable with what bubbles up, and when we invite into our thoughts the things that make us happy—a special child in our life, moments of joy while playing a sport, images of nature, warm childhood memories, a project we are envisioning—we begin to create a safe space for ourselves within ourselves. We get lost in the beauty of our thoughts, and our imagination comes alive. The parts of us that get drowned out amid the noise of life have a chance to speak. We can hear the downloads that connect us to our purpose; we understand how we can add good to the world. While our purpose finds its expression and fulfillment in community, we cannot show up as our best for others if we are not tending to ourselves first. The quiet moments that precede the togetherness, the solitary reflection that happens in between the wonderful communion with others, is essential for alignment. (I share more about the care and nurturing of ourselves in chapter 6.) We are more than one thing and meant to do many incredible things over our lives.

We're all on different journeys and in different stages of exploration and execution of purpose, in part because we're always evolving and assignments may be overlapping. You can be in alignment with your purpose now and looking to take your successes and gifts to the next level, to widen your community and your business influence and scale up. Or you may have detoured from alignment and are looking to correct course. Or perhaps you're searching for a community with whom you can discover your purpose and passion. And sometimes, our assignments shift midstream, calling us to move in a direction and toward a purpose we had never considered or even imagined.

The most important thing about your purpose is that it brings you and your community together and that it provides joy and a sense of fulfillment. If you are a nanny and you love what you do, there is purpose there, for you are using your gifts to care tenderly for a child in a way that pays lifelong dividends. If you are a Little League coach, there is a purpose in what you are doing that goes beyond recreation—you are catching kids early on in life and instilling confidence and teaching them what it means to be part of a team. If you are running a food truck business on the weekends to serve families in your neighborhood or building your financial tech company to serve people who don't have access to mainstream banking services, there is great purpose there—you are lending your energy and vibration for the greater good. Pockets of everyday purpose are just as important as big-picture purpose, because so often those pockets blossom into something more far-reaching than what we could have initially envisioned. The more responsive we are to assignments, the more authentic and aligned we become, and the more our purpose is revealed to us.

Believe me, I still have challenging moments. Staying attuned to purpose is ongoing work, and one of my ways of staying grounded is by expressing gratitude for the things that are going well. This helps me identify the small and not-so-small things that bring me joy and that I want more of in my life (and it helps me identify the areas where I might need to make some changes). You can also ask friends or family members what they see as your greatest strengths, or your superpower. The people who love us and know us best can see gifts in us that we may not recognize. In periods of lethargy or being generally stuck, it's easy to be hard on yourself and thus be unable to see the things that make you great.

As a kid, I would lie with my siblings on a quilt that we'd spread across the grass, and we would watch the clouds move across the sky. I had a vivid imagination (still do) and would make up whole stories about what the clouds were doing, what life was like up there, how an existence in that realm offered a different, sometimes better life, filled with unlimited opportunities, where anything was possible. This simple act of imaginary creation is the spark from which real creations grow. Every thing, every business, every purpose is born first as an idea in the mind's eye. As an adult, it's easy to lose that spark, but it's important to keep visualizing and dreaming—why not take a blanket to the nearest park and lie down for a while, manifesting what you want? By allowing yourself that time to relax and tap into creativity, you might be surprised at what you find.

And then, of course, there is community.

Our passions gain momentum when we intersect with others who are following their assignments, and the energy of being around like-minded villagers is so powerful. I often think back to Mrs. E. encouraging me to take the special education certification exam; even though I had no idea where that would lead, I trusted her instincts that it might come in handy one day. And when I realized just *how* useful that certification was, I was incredibly grateful to be seen so well by her.

The internal work you do as you explore your gifts and build up the belief in yourself gives you the confidence to share space in your community, to see another person's gifts and not be intimidated by them. It allows you to operate authentically in community, to fill a role where one is needed, to accept help and advice from others and to give it. A big part of this work is to build yourself up, and it's something that even the greatest achievers must do. As an entrepreneur and business owner, and especially as a person of color, you have to build yourself up every day. You must have an unwavering belief in your ability and trust what you've been called to do or called to create.

One of my favorite athletes and racial and social justice advocates is Muhammad Ali. Some found his confidence and boasting annoying and said that he needed humility. I saw it differently—I believe that we got to witness his internal dialogue being shared out loud. We got to hear how he talked himself up to be prepared for all that he'd face as Cassius, a Black man from Kentucky who grew up during a time of racial segregation. He had to transform himself into a warrior of an athlete, and we got to experience his affirmations along with him, adorning his spirit with words of greatness, deflecting mediocrity so that he could truly become and be great. He is immortalized as one of the greatest athletes to have ever lived, and we saw him fight against the odds and to speak against that quiet voice that exists in all of us, a voice that can be loud if we let it, a voice that tells us to be afraid and that we can only go so far. He shouted against that voice and what we heard was, "I am the greatest," and he worked toward that greatness, which we all had an opportunity to witness.

I get why people might find this behavior annoying, but there's a powerful lesson here: It's important to shout louder than that internal voice telling you that you can't do something. Success does not happen without consistent work and a voice loudly affirming that we are meant for greatness, that we have purpose, and that we embody everything we need to become exactly who we are meant to be. Sometimes you have to be that loud voice for yourself. And once you gather your village, I promise that they, too, will use their voices to lift you up, and you them.

When we all come together and bring our authentic selves, guided by purpose, greater things happen than can happen alone. I believe that you have to meet and be connected to other people to do the Big Thing, that in order to complete your assignment, it must be done with others, whether it's with a couple of other people or many. One of Ali's greatest friends and confidants was one of my personal heroes and favorite leaders, Malcolm X, a charismatic and influential civil rights leader who advocated for Black empowerment and liberation from systemic oppression. They bonded over their faith and commitment to social justice. Malcolm X was a safe space and reassuring voice for Ali as he navigated the complexities of self-discovery, stardom, and being a voice for social justice issues.

Wherever you are in your entrepreneurship journey, your life journey, in discovering your purpose and saying yes to your assignments, you must build and lean into your community, your beloved village. All the people I highlighted in this chapter who embraced their purpose attracted a team of believers who contributed their own unique gifts toward the mission.

## Reflection Questions

* Which parts of your life feel energizing, and which feel depleting? When you consider your purpose and business plan, how can you use those energizing elements to help guide you?

* Can you remember a time when your life was out of alignment? What are the signs that you should've exited that assignment sooner?

* If you are still unsure whether you are moving in alignment and purpose as an entrepreneur, consider what your friends and family come to you for advice or help with. What does that tell you about which assignments you should be saying yes to or seeking out?

* When was the last time you noticed a problem in your community and felt compelled to solve it? How did you solve it?

* What makes you feel energized outside of work?

* Looking back on your life, can you identify decisions you made that were life assignments? What domino effect did those yeses have?

# THREE

# Roll Call
## Building Your Village

NEARLY A DECADE AGO, HAVING JUST KICKED OFF THE VILLAGE Market, I was invited to a back-to-school panel in Atlanta. There I was introduced to another panelist, city councilor Andre Dickens. He had a huge smile on his face and radiated warmth as he shook my hand, and we quickly bonded over our love for children, education, and community. Standing well over six feet, his towering presence could easily have felt intimidating, but the children and their parents gravitated to him. He was present and at ease, and there was a real kindness to how he asked questions and listened intently, connecting authentically with each person he spoke to. We promised to stay in touch and support each other for the betterment of our community—and even early on, I felt confident we would.

Andre lived up to his word. As the Village Market grew, Andre was there as an enthusiast, injecting positivity into every interaction. He always said yes to my invitations, even attending our "Support Is a Verb" campaign kickoff, a fun photoshoot event rooted in inspiring the community to embrace intentional actions and collectivism.

When I attended community gatherings outside the Village Market—whether it was a grassroots function or a meeting with corporate leaders—Andre was there, too, talking to everyone. As a councilor, he prioritized community-first issues such as affordable housing and safe schools and neighborhoods, always seeking to weave everyone together, no matter their political faction. This was clearly not a man who bought into the self-made myth. In fact, he often spoke about the way forward using the analogy of a circle, which connects everyone, as opposed to drawing lines, which can create barriers. In addition to seeing him as the ultimate enthusiast and supporter, I also viewed him as a visionary, as a leader who energized others and made them believe that something greater was possible with collaboration.

Early one morning in 2019, during my morning prayer ritual to set my intentions for the day, my mind randomly went to Andre. I saw his vibrant smile and his believable, warm spirit. I was deep into the building phase of my business at the time—we'd gone from a little word-of-mouth event to becoming part of the fabric of Atlanta—and as the village model was creating sustainable prosperity for Black entrepreneurs and we touched more lives, I became increasingly desirous of a city leader who could steer Atlanta forward communally, who could run that extension cord through every community, empowering every villager. I had a crystal-clear vision of Andre's role—leading the city as our next mayor.

I wasn't sure if Andre had seriously considered himself for this consequential role—though he had talked about his boyhood dream of becoming mayor—but I felt so moved by what I envisioned that I had to reach out. I am someone who trusts two things above all else: what I feel and the visions that I have. So I sent Andre a message: "I pray that you are one day our mayor. When the time comes, I'm right by your side. It really seems like it's your destiny. So keep doing the good work and aligning your village because we will be ready." He responded that he was honored to receive my message and that yes, he had the same hopes. I felt excited that he also held this bigger vision and purpose for himself, and even though the thought had crossed my mind randomly, I started my day with a great sense of calm and conviction that he'd one day be the mayor of Atlanta.

Just two years later, I sat glued to my television, watching the 2021 Atlanta mayoral debate. There, center stage, was Andre. The front-runners, two seasoned politicians, stood at their podiums, delivering their arguments with an assuredness, as if there was absolutely no question in their mind they'd be the next mayor. Even though Andre was polling low at that point, I was thrilled he was in the race. But I felt uneasy. It wasn't the other candidates' confidence that had me on edge but that they seemed to deem Andre as a noncompetitor, though he had done so much for our community. He had won two citywide races since 2013, but the other candidates appeared to be writing him off—interrupting him, ignoring him, treating him (because he was trailing in the polls) like he didn't stand a chance.

As the debate went on, I listened as Andre answered questions thoughtfully and passionately, at one point using his hands to make his characteristic circle, representing his vision of a mayorship that would embrace all corridors and communities of Atlanta. There was no question in my mind that Andre was the best candidate for the job. In all my time running the Village Market, he was the only council member who had shown up to our events, and with nothing to gain at that point—no votes, no press, no accolades. I'd witnessed how he created opportunities for the most vulnerable—youth, seniors, people at a skills disadvantage in our ever-increasing high-tech work environment. In 2018, he'd founded a tech nonprofit to do just that. He valued entrepreneurs and small-business owners, as he'd been one himself. I knew that if people did not take this election seriously, this man who never missed our community-driven events would not become mayor.

That night, I sent Andre a simple text: "What do you need?" He answered that he needed support from the people who believed in him to get his message out.

OK, I thought. Game on.

He needed connectors, people to bring together the right people into roles that would create movement for Team Andre. In the years since I'd launched the Village Market, I'd nurtured a good number of relationships with talented people who could put their faith in me and hence in him. I am not often someone who makes her politics public, but I am someone who is public about her belief in community; I figured that if I could help put him on people's radars, they could make the decision for themselves. Honestly, I was confident that once they heard his vision, they would want to cast their ballot for a Mayor Dickens.

True to my promise from two years prior—that the village would be ready—I reached out to a bunch of friends and colleagues to get the word out and strategize how to raise awareness. How could this trusted network use their gifts and villages to lift up this extraordinary candidate? They all stepped up. My friend Zack, who owns the Local Green restaurant, had been an early advocate for Andre's candidacy and agreed to collaborate on amplifying his platform. My fellow community builders—Ryan Wilson, CEO of the Gathering Spot (a community hub and a private entrepreneur membership club), J. Carter, CEO of ONE Musicfest, and renowned artist Fahuma Pécou—shared their ideas and contacts to widen the village of folks we could bring onto "Team Dre." We created a social campaign and event, Great Day in Atlanta (modeled on Great Day in Harlem), to bring influencers, community leaders, business owners, and everyday people together to understand Andre's mission. From there, we planned back-to-back events to energize the voting base, including a Get Out to Vote concert that included Atlanta legends Goodie Mob and T.I. The response was overwhelmingly positive. While the economic, political, and social risk of backing the long-shot candidate was real, what I noticed was that people really resonated with a candidate focused on community.

More and more people reached out asking how they could spread the word and help others find the courage to stand with Andre and to commit to drawing circles and erasing lines. The Team Dre group text grew; he garnered support from many successful founders and well-known artists, restaurateurs, community strategists, and activists who publicly endorsed him.

The common thread that linked many of us to Andre was that he had supported us all at some point or another. Even the people who hadn't been familiar with his work could see how beautiful and far-reaching the impact was once they'd been introduced to it. We trusted that he'd hold the city with delicate hands and mold his circle thoughtfully with every type of resident in mind. What made this effort the most gratifying was how we worked together and volunteered our networks, talents, and platforms: We fundraised and lent marketing support, without ego or competition, in whatever role was needed, and we pooled our collective gifts and resources so that the better candidate for the people of Atlanta could win. This powerful (albeit temporary) village was built passionately and in record time to solve a community need.

On November 30, two years to the day that I hit send on that prescient message, Andre Dickens won the mayoral race by the largest margin in Atlanta's history. That night, I logged on to IG and posted a photo of us hugging, along with a screenshot of the message I'd sent him two years earlier. "Much love," he responded, "my first comment as Mayor Elect goes to you."

WHEN WE CREATE or enter into a community guided by our purpose, magic happens. The night that Andre won, the village won. Many people met up at the Gathering Spot, sharing hugs, tears, and excitement. Those of us who celebrated from our homes Facetimed together, lighting up our group chats with champagne emojis and texts in all caps. Our guy won—he did it. *We* did it. We came together and served our unique roles. Collective efforts won. A vision for a greater Atlanta felt more and more real and many of us felt more connected, not just to our city, but to our power center: the community.

When I set out to create the Village Market, I began to understand how important it is to have people on your team who serve in unique roles, people who can contribute with ease what a moment or project calls for, whether it's relationship building, big-vision thinking, or utilizing their talent to champion the work. A role is based on your skills, but it isn't *limited* to your skills. At its heart, a role is relationship based. It's the unique patch you provide to complete the quilt. We all are born with qualities that might naturally fit a certain role better than others, and those roles can shift based on the communities we are in. That said, filling a role does not lessen your individuality—you should not have to dim your light or any aspects of yourself that are valuable parts of who you are.

The six roles that follow are ones I believe every community project or business can benefit from as it gets off the ground or soars into its next phase. Depending on where someone is in their entrepreneurial journey, they may need to prioritize certain roles over others or serve in multiple roles. There have also been countless times when I and my team members are called to step into different shoes depending on the task at hand. Roles are not entirely fixed—you are not just one thing. Life challenges us to be more or less of something depending on the circumstances and the mission. The beautiful thing about a village mentality is that people are able to embrace a role where it's needed in the moment for the greater good.

When I am hiring, I consider someone's traits and discover what sparks passion for them. I ask what feels easy or challenging for them, and I take the information and begin designing where they'd fit best in the company and who they should be paired with on the team. While a community really is "all hands on deck," the true power of the community is that not every hand is doing the same thing. A community in which everyone is a leader is not going to do very well because you need a diversity of skills and roles in service of the bigger purpose. I tell my team members, friends, and mentees: "Engage in the area that you are most talented in. We need your passion there."

## THE FUTURIST

Futurists might be the first type of personality that comes to mind when you think of entrepreneurship. They're the people who see things beyond the present, things that most folks don't, and figure out how to change the way others see the world and one another. Martin Luther King Jr. is a shining example of a futurist. He made us believe in his dream of racial equality, taking us there in his mind. Futurists can always see a bigger picture, looking beyond an idea and how it can influence their community once complete. They often have extraordinary charm that attracts people to listen and believe in the message and the vision. Importantly, while futurists have the ability to see beyond what currently exists, they are also credible and have clarity of thought so that their dreams feel real and accessible. There's an element of practicality there. Barack Obama has this gift—he is charismatic and believable; he can communicate his vision that change is possible, then back it up with concrete steps to get there.

I am often the futurist on my team, and when I collaborate with other futurists, we strive to accomplish what we see and know is possible. When I birthed the idea for the Village Market—and later for the Village Retail and my nonprofit, Our Village United—I saw the finished product as clearly as I could look out the window and see a building or a bird in flight. I knew I had to articulate that vision for entrepreneurs so they could feel it was being built for them. I showed them, step-by-step, that it could be done.

Not every person is a natural-born futurist. It is a unique gift in the same way that being a painter or a musician is. The truest sign of being a futurist is that when you look at an empty lot, you don't notice the vacancy—instead, you see what can fill that lot, whether it's a playground with kids running around or a restaurant serving the neighborhood. With that vision in mind, you lead the way toward it. Looking back at my childhood and young adulthood, I see glimpses of my futurist role, small things that prepared me for the larger steps I'd later take. The summer after I graduated from college, I was sitting outside under the carport of my grandmother Josephine's house, watching a bunch of kids in the street hanging around, not doing much. There wasn't a rec center in this neighborhood, and I figured these kids were bound to get into trouble if they didn't have something to engage them. An idea grabbed me. "I want to write a play and get all kids and the community involved," I told my grandmother. These youngsters were the ones who didn't get chosen for anything, and they probably hadn't had a lot of opportunities come across their paths. This would give them a sense of belonging and fuel their purpose. "Do it," she said, and she didn't need to say it twice; I was already off and running. First I wrote a play about young people finding their way. Then I gathered the kids and told them we'd be doing this together (they were timid but excited) and that we had to rehearse daily at the local church (hey, I sneakily got them to go to church). We packed the church for an end-of-summer performance, and the entire neighborhood turned out. It was incredible. A few years ago, I received a message from one of the teens—now a grown man—thanking me for getting him off the streets that summer.

To this day, my ideas and visions pull me with such a force that I can't *not* do it—I can't shake it, even if it intimidates me. The best part, really, is being able to actualize ideas that impact the community. All leaders have a choice for how they will use their gifts.

Community-oriented futurists must actively choose, daily, to operate with village-made values (which I discuss in the next chapter).
Otherwise, this gift, this prescient sense of future planning, can lead
a person's motivations astray. There have been too many futurists
throughout history who have used their talents for self-aggrandizing
purposes, who have built their visions on models of hierarchy and
exclusion—dictators who use charm to manipulate others into doing
their bidding, even when the dictator only has their own well-being
in mind. Livelihoods and actual lives depend on having futurists
who lead from a place of equity and inclusion, who ask themselves,
"Who will I be to the community?"

While not everyone needs to be a futurist for their company or
community, everyone has the ability to be imaginative and to create. We are all born with that impulse. As children we lived in our
imaginations and created whole worlds. Writing that play for the
youth that one summer helped me tap into mine! It's tricky because
as adults, due to stress or disappointments or life choices, that instinct gets muddled or tucked away. But the ability to teleport ourselves to different worlds in our minds doesn't go away. If you are
looking to flex your imagination muscle, take time to daydream
and create, even on a small scale—planning a charity drive for coworkers or spearheading a group work project you've dreamed up.
Having an idea or a vision and seeing it come to fruition with others brings a beautiful feeling of purpose. Some futurists (including
myself) practice vision casting, an exercise where you close your
eyes, leave this moment, and intentionally experience the future
as you dream it. If you want to create a logo for your business, for
example, you imagine not only the logo but also where it will live
and the partnerships you'll have because of it. This detailed, unlimited vision serves as the attainable goal that you work toward.
I totally nerded out when I recently learned from a science writer
friend that our brains are built to assist us in daydreaming: We are

neurologically wired with a default mode network that lights up when we are remembering, thinking about the future, or thinking creatively (it also lights up when we are practicing empathy and socializing).

## THE BUILDER

Builders are the people who make things happen. They listen to other people's visions and goals, think it over, and say, "This is how to do it." As you might guess, they don't stay in the ideation phase long—they are action oriented and have a willingness to get to work. If a park needs to be built, they build it. When someone on the team is sick and needs a meal train, they create it. Grassroots organizations making big changes in the community are fueled by builders. Our history is filled with people who embody the builder role, verb-oriented folks who see a deprivation and move to fill it. When I began looking for Black female entrepreneur role models, I read about Maggie Lena Walker, the first African American woman—and the first woman—to found a bank in the United States, the St. Luke Penny Savings, which opened in 1903. The daughter of enslaved parents, Walker had an acuity for finances and an unwavering belief that in order for Black communities to thrive, members needed to do business with an institution free from the rampant racism in the banking industry that denied Black business owners loans or charged them sky-high interest rates. She also understood that creating a Black-owned bank would consolidate economic power by keeping money and profits circulating in the Black community. So what did she do? She hired Black employees and issued hundreds of business loans and mortgages for home ownership. The bank was one of the few to survive the Great Depression, and today it is still in operation (having consolidated with two larger banks). Like many builders, Walker was also a futurist—she saw the end product and worked toward it. Combining those two roles often leads to towering achievements. When I have worked with fellow builders, I love how we are able to lock in on the mission. We get things done. We celebrate meeting our goals and we trust each other to get things done.

Builders can be take-charge leaders or they can sit back and let a futurist take the lead—or they can work in tandem. Really, all they need are the tools to execute the vision; they can either take direction from a futurist or come up with the blueprint on their own. I'd say that the best builders are those who can pull strengths out of the collaborators—those important folks who are glad to chip in wherever they are needed—to organize the village to fulfill the assignment efficiently. Just like great coaches, they can see the team and which positions to place people in. Similar to futurists, they must be believable in order to gain the team's trust, and they must also be open to taking constructive feedback. Builders serve as excellent number twos in an organization not only because they can step into a leadership role if need be but also because they can take on some of the logistical work and free up the futurist to do more big-picture thinking.

In the early stages of a business, it may be necessary for futurists to embody the role of builder as well. Even folks who are a part of a larger organization can step into the role of builder in their day-to-day capacities. Every time you organize a meeting, launch a project, or write a proposal, you are building, creating a framework and piecing together what's needed to bring something to fruition. One of the most beautiful parts of being a builder, I think, is the way you seek out the talents of everyone in the village and collaborate with them. Aside from benefiting from the futurist's ideas and the collaborators' actions, builders often rely on connectors, those who are talented at recognizing the unique way each villager can contribute to an assignment.

# THE CONNECTOR

Wired to *see* the abilities of different people and what can happen if they work together, connectors are a special and essential part of the village. Let's say a connector walks into a room and sees person A, a brilliant carpenter, and person B, an entrepreneur seeking to build new shelving in their coffee shop. Without thinking much about it, the connector would be aware of this mutually beneficial situation and communicate what could happen if they were to collaborate. I like to think of them as bridge builders. It's incredible how connectors recognize talents in people and how those gifts can be strengthened when connected to another person. Connectors are also adept at maintaining a good number of genuine relationships at one time—they are open, curious, and people loving (though they must be careful to reserve time for self-care so they don't get socially tapped out). Because connectors are discerning and naturally tuned in to a person's authenticity, their invitations are usually trustworthy and safe. To be a connector, I believe you must have a certain level of emotional intelligence. This allows you to empathize with people on a deep level and see past the surface.

Another brilliant thing about connectors is that along with being able to see how people fit together, they are also adept at *eliminating* the things that keep people separated. They get rid of the distractions and tools of separation—political labels, generational stereotypes, racial constructs—that keep villagers from singing from the same hymnal. Connectors play on #TeamBoth. You can revere both Malcolm X and Martin Luther King Jr., even though their approaches to social justice are somewhat distinct.

You have probably served as a connector in your work life at one point or another, perhaps recommending someone for a job or asking a person on your team to mentor someone else because you sensed they would pair well together. I am often playing connector in my work, and I have benefited from those in the connector role as well.

It's one of the most rewarding positions to be in, giving people the gift of others who can help them along their path!

# THE COLLABORATOR

Collaborators assist the builders. Collaborators don't need or necessarily want to lead a mission, but they are there faithfully to help execute it. While collaborators don't often seek the limelight (they prefer to help chip away at Mount Rushmore, not be the face on it), they deserve it—the world cannot run without them. During the pandemic, we saw how the country's collaborators, our essential workers, kept the economy going, educated our children under trying conditions, and risked their lives as health-care workers. Collaborators are the unsung heroes of many "self-made" stories.

Collaborators are wonderful at sharing space and fulfilling a shared mission. When I hire collaborators, I know that I can count on them to go over and beyond to see a task completed. They consistently show up and want to get their hands dirty, whether it's making phone calls, picking up supplies, or creating invites. They are the ones who are happy to go out and get the ribbon so that someone else can cut it. Because collaborators are likely to say yes most of the time, it's important that those who rely on their trustworthiness do not take advantage of their willingness. When I have worked with collaborators, often the task is helping them *not* say yes all the time, to create boundaries for themselves and tune in to their personal cues for burnout so they don't take on too much. Futurists and builders should develop an awareness of when they are asking too much of collaborators, for collaborators rarely wear their exhaustion on their sleeve (it's part of their nature to try hard *not* to look tired). It's also important for leaders to regularly thank and reward collaborators. Collaborators are not looking for thank-yous—they are happy to clap for others and make sure leaders have what they need—but they deserve to know how important they are for the village and to feel the love.

# THE ENTHUSIAST

This is the person you call with your best news and your worst. Enthusiasts make people feel safe and supported, and they truly love the role they serve: affirming those in their community. Because they are locked in to their mission and the talents of those around them, they are consistent, unwavering pillars of support. The only thing they ask of you is to be great, to be the amazing person they know you to be. They proudly stand by your side and believe in you, even on your worst days, when they'll probably tell you, "Shrug it off; it's just a bad day." We all have to build ourselves up daily, and having an enthusiast in our corner helps us do that. Enthusiasts are deeply in tune with others—they are empathic and intuitive and can feel another person's energy—and their timing always feels right (there's nothing like getting that random call or text just when you need it). And while enthusiasts and connectors both possess empathy, the difference is that an enthusiast's main relationship is with you and your immediate team, whereas connectors are nimbly navigating many relationships in different sectors. My sister Yolanda is the epitome of an enthusiast—she thinks I'm amazing, and when I need the reminder most, I rely on her unwavering belief in my talents to remind me of who I am and why I do what I do.

When I have hired enthusiasts, they bring good energy to the team. If I am excited about a new idea or project, I typically tell them first so that we can build momentum together. Since enthusiasts are so committed to the purpose—they want the win!—they're able to offer thoughtful, constructive feedback and bring a sense of positivity to hard projects, reminding the community of the beautiful, prosperous dream we're seeking to achieve. In addition to their deep faith in community, they have a respect for the roles everyone plays. And because they're so skilled at appreciating the work that others do, they make the community that much closer.

I have inhabited the role of enthusiast—for myself and others— many times over the years. I imagine most entrepreneurs have. Building a successful business is like running back-to-back marathons, and you must be able to step back and remind yourself—and others— what and why you're building. When my team was struggling in the final stages before a Village Market event, I gathered them to remind them why we were working so hard: "Soon people from all over— Atlanta, Detroit, Los Angeles, Mississippi—will gather, and they will see and experience Black businesses and artisans from all over the country, selling the finest products. They will take selfies, they will dance, and many will eat vegan food for the first time. Children will walk in and their eyes will widen and they'll ask with excitement, 'Is this Wakanda?' Elders will weep because they will remember a time when a celebration like this was not allowed. They will see the fruits of their sacrifices and remember when they had to dim their Blackness and their light. At the end of the night, with a sense of safety, inclusion, representation, Black joy and commerce, they will remember the village; they will remember you."

## THE OBSERVER

Observers see a thing for what it is and bring it into sharper focus. These folks have an incredible ability to read a room, to hear a story, and to pull out the things that matter most. They bring a critical eye, but they are also protective and loving. Elders are sometimes in the role of observers due to their wisdom and life experience. We trust them because we know that when they speak, they have our best interests at heart and they can see with a wide lens. When I work with observers, I know the protection and overall purpose is always top of mind. Observers hold the mission close and are great at figuring out what to dial up (or cut back on) to achieve it. Often, you'll see observers serving on boards (including Our Village United), where they counsel on big-picture issues. You might also find them in marketing roles, where they excel at figuring out the important information to build a campaign.

Observers are incredible at distilling what's important and worth paying attention to in our culture. Artists of all kinds—writers, painters, musicians, sculptors—fulfill this role beautifully, using art to truth-tell and to give voice to the unspoken—the glorious and the ugly—in ways that demand our attention, compelling us to look at and *feel* what is happening in our midst and to act. The writers James Baldwin and Maya Angelou and the singer Nina Simone are people who embody the power of the observer. Baldwin's writings on economic and racial inequality shake the reader into a deep understanding of the full humanity of Black people and the awfulness of white supremacy, urging a path toward racial harmony and a world without oppression. His ability to speak fearlessly about issues, no matter the audience or arena, inspires me to do the same. He provides a loud critique and observation of the Black experience and challenges for different outcomes. Maya Angelou's poems and memoirs are a form of keen observation and activism, riveting the reader with language that ignites emotion, empathy, and critical thought, inspiring us to live with purpose and compassion. Nina Simone's soulful voice washes over listeners in ways that makes them feel deeply. Her "Mississippi Goddamn," a response to the racially motivated killing of Medgar Evers and the bombing of the 16th Street Baptist Church, which killed four young Black girls (and blinded a fifth), carries the pain of racial oppression and ignites an urgency to stamp it out. It marked the beginning of Simone's journey as a civil rights activist, and her powerful songs have since moved many to expand their social and political consciousness. All three allowed the times to be their muse and provided a voice to people who were often voiceless. Artists are creators, and so, I believe, are entrepreneurs. Your art is your venture. Your business is your canvas.

WE NEED ONE another in order to step into the greatness of our talents and our roles, to pull ourselves up not by our own bootstraps but with the strength of others, arm in arm. A futurist cannot lead without builders, and a builder cannot build without collaborators. Businesses cannot grow without connectors, and connectors have no one to connect if individuals are not discovering their purpose and accepting their assignments.

Regardless of the role you are embodying or the assignment in front of you, a flourishing village requires that everyone prioritize the relationships of those doing the work. No mission succeeds if the connections between villagers are not nurtured and intentionally guided by village-made values, those that are rooted in respect, compassion, and commitment.

## Reflection Questions

★ Of the six team roles described in this chapter, which one or two do you most identify with? Why?

★ What roles do you think someone else in your business should fill in order to complement your strengths?

★ Which roles do you want to grow in? Is there someone in your business you could learn from?

★ Are there employees who might benefit from learning the ropes of a role they are not currently in or who show potential to grow into a different role?

# FOUR

# Village-Made Values

A FEW YEARS AGO, I WAS MEANDERING THROUGH A SMALL street fair in Atlanta, taking in the colorful kaleidoscope of wares and the sounds of children giggling as they ran by. I smiled at a few people who were dancing in front of the DJ booth to Afrobeat. As I smelled a couple of candles at one booth, my eyes gravitated to a guy across the aisle wearing a black T-shirt with bold white letters: *All Black Lives Matter. And I mean all.* I walked over to his booth where the shirts were for sale, reading the words again—they mirrored what my heart felt. *This* was what I was trying to do with my business. It deeply resonated with my belief as a village builder and businesswoman. I build for *all* Black businesses that are well-intentioned and aligned on the mission, who are sharing their gifts toward the greater goal of the collective. I don't exclude based on the number of followers a business owner has, how much money or the level of experience they bring to the table, or how "connected" they are. My day-to-day life is steeped in the belief that all business owners are seen, respected, and welcomed. This overarching value—that all

Black lives matter—guides me as I build. I believe that aggressive inclusivity is the only way we will build enough to achieve sustainable racial and economic parity. Only when everyone is considered does everyone have a lane to prosperity.

When I launched the Village Market, I committed to creating a business that reflected this basic belief in every aspect, from the small decisions to the big ones. As I built, I uncovered some capital-K Key values that have kept my approach to business firmly in the community and inclusivity lane, with guardrails to prevent drift into self-made territory. I define values as *the beliefs that a leader embodies as they build their business and work with others.* These village-made values nurture and guide the work and the relationships of those doing the work. They are ones that I believe should be baked into any enterprise committed to a community-centered approach. These values have enabled each of my companies to be equitable, impactful, and, importantly, profitable (in chapter 7, I discuss economic structures that help you to turn a profit while still staying true to the community). They defy the myth of self-made and move us forward with a mindset of togetherness.

In reality, all companies—not just mine—have values that determine and reflect how they do business. Whether these values are spoken or unspoken, they exist, seeped throughout the decision-making. Even when business owners haven't consciously identified values, their day-to-day choices—from hiring to managing to budgeting to customer service—reveal what they deem worthy and what is dismissed. Values are not inherently good or bad. But typically under capitalism, companies operate with profit-over-people values. With that model, employee well-being simply can't be the priority. For that reason, without clear, intentional, and *community-minded* values, it's all too easy to conform to dogmatic approaches that support the individual (the owner, the shareholder, the investor) but do not advance and sustain the community or the staff. Carefully considered and specific values help guide how you relate to your team, your customers, and your community as you prosper. Profit isn't sidelined, but neither will it crowd out one of the main reasons you are building: to stimulate and vitalize the village. Another way to think about village values is in terms of the workplace culture. Workplace culture is how people behave according to a set of spoken and unspoken beliefs—it's "the way things are done." And research finds it matters. A lot. Employees who say their work culture is positive are nearly four times more likely to be engaged in their jobs. Employees describe a positive work culture as one that is supportive, inclusive, flexible, caring, collaborative, and innovative—the very values that speak to how people should show up for one another while they do the work. What this tells me is that when a leader cares about how their team members are experiencing their workplace, those employees actually perform better. But these values do not materialize without futurists who are deliberate about braiding them into every aspect of the organization, nor without employees who are invested in upholding them. People in leadership roles—futurists, builders, and connectors—are in a unique and privileged position to establish a workplace culture and values that nourish the mission and team relationships.

There are many paths to building a successful village, so the list of values that follows is by no means complete. Certainly, there are values that are specific to each entrepreneur and mission. This is why it is so important to do self-exploration—you need to identify what matters most to you. But these six values are my anchors; they keep my feet planted on the ground as I look up and build ahead. They root my actions, my mindset, and my relationships in the village.

1. **Share space with people who shine in areas you don't.** One of the best pieces of advice my grandmothers, Bobbi and Josephine, gave me—and that I have consistently heard on my journey—was *surround yourself with people who are more talented than you are.* When I was laying the groundwork

for my nonprofit, Our Village United, I invited talented and diverse speakers and founders who had different gifts than my own. This was critical, as I knew that a deep bench of experts would help catapult the success of the solopreneurs we were targeting, the 96 percent of single-operator Black business owners (in contrast, 81 percent of white business owners are single operators). Before I officially launched my nonprofit, I piloted a niche group of ten entrepreneurs who were ready to grow their concepts. I had already gotten to know them from the Urban Grind speaker series I curated, and I saw they were talented and driven. I was excited about having a closer relationship with the entrepreneurs to better understand their challenges, to take on a role of observer.

So with nothing more than a shared dream and a goal to see it through together, our little village started meeting on Saturdays at a neighborhood tea shop, Honey Bubble. We gathered around a small meeting table and began to flesh out their business ideas. I listened carefully to the discussions. I jumped into conversations, guiding the novice business owners to set intentions for what they desired for themselves. I primed them with talk about community and setting a village mindset. "Let's all put our heads together for Kim!" While the sharing was a wonderful way to kick off the project, I quickly recognized that they needed more expertise than I could provide. So I decided to bring people into this endeavor who could offer what I could not—branding and marketing advice, business plan know-how, budgeting chops, product development.

Opening the doors to outside contributors may seem like a no-brainer, but I have since discovered that not all leaders are quick to bring in collaborators when they are needed. This goes back to a scarcity mindset, in which many leaders worry that the presence of others will lessen their own potential impact. I believe the inability to be vulnerable has handicapped many a leader's ability to grow and scale what could be profitable and impactful enterprises. The reality is that you have to respect your own limitations. These budding entrepreneurs had put their trust in me—a woman who was just starting to grow her own business!—so I felt obligated, and frankly excited, to connect them with the mentors they needed to flourish. And I was learning too. As someone who has never believed in the notion of self-made, it was a necessity and a privilege to usher in those who could help support the group mission and move it forward.

Now, as a leader, it was my responsibility to bring in the *right* people, those who were mission aligned, to make sure the experts who'd be sharing space with us were committed to mentoring Black business owners. As the Saturdays passed, trusted volunteer facilitators (some of whom I'd tapped for the Urban Grind speaker series) showed up to teach classes in everything from branding to marketing. It was amazing to witness the business owners working collaboratively as they shared ideas and connected with the facilitators. (Transparency and generosity with knowledge are a must for the village. Sharing skillsets is incredibly valuable!) It felt like I was still in a classroom setting, but it looked a little different—instead of discussing short stories and essay writing, we were talking about building and envisioning and scaling from the seats of the intimate and mighty microvillage that we'd created.

This little village was my first business incubator test group, my launch pad for what would become my nonprofit's national program ELEVATE, a twelve-week program dedicated to supporting Black entrepreneurs as they think through their operations and infrastructure with the end goal of scaling up. I have continued to forge beautiful and loving relationships with other futurists over the years, people I am honored to usher into Our Village United—friends and colleagues like Severti Wilson, an innovative community nonprofit founder in the technology space, and my dear friend Eunique Jones Gibson, a genius serial entrepreneur and content-creation unicorn who believes in the village model. While it is easy to find high-net-worth entrepreneurs, my commitment is to bring in those who lead with a social impact model, who lift as they climb.

Many of the entrepreneurs in that original group have benefited hugely from the array of mentoring. When I opened the Village Retail in 2020, Kim's wonderful essential oils were on the shelves—she'd gone from a DIYer to a scaled-up business owner. DJ Boogie Lov has grown to DJ for President Biden, Stacey Abrams, and more. None of this would have been possible had it not been for my continued willingness to invite in superb people who could contribute what I could not. And none of this would have materialized had those generous village-minded experts not said yes to my invitation to share their experiences and knowledge.

It takes a deep level of self-awareness and confidence to be motivated by others' talents rather than intimidated by them, but in order to build a community of excellence, we need to be able to identify our weaknesses and bring in those who complete the quilt, those who can add the missing pieces. Their excellence will also challenge you to up your game. Iron sharpens iron.

2. **Ask for help. And help others.** There is power in being vulnerable and asking for help. It brings you closer to people. It lets them know that you are human, and your willingness to admit that you need help models the essential truth that you cannot and should not do everything alone. Asking

for an assist also gives villagers the opportunity to step up
and contribute for the greater good, which is, after all, the
point of a village. I've experienced this truth over and over,
but I had to relearn it in a big way when the Village Market
really took off. As the germ of my idea for elevated market
events blossomed, and as more tasks presented themselves,
I felt increasingly guilty asking my team, who were mostly
volunteering at that point, to do even more. I felt that they
had not signed up for the idea to grow as quickly as it was.
I retreated from their offers of support and took on more
tasks myself—securing event spaces, working directly with
contractors, designing the floor layout—not because I didn't
trust them with those tasks but because I did not want them
to feel obliged. I have always felt an uneasiness about asking
for too much help and never want people to feel obligated to
support me. It took many sessions with my therapist—who
heard the raw truth of how overwhelmed I was—to help
me identify that people love to get behind good ideas, and
when people have trust in a person, it feels purposeful, not
obligatory. Once I had this revelation, I vowed to be very
honest with my little volunteer village, especially with Danyel,
Kris, Courtney, Carol, and Nadia, who were my core group
of support. I called a meeting and let them know that I was
pulled thin. Because I was still working at GADOE (and in
the throes of my mission misalignment, if you recall), I was
barely sleeping as I strove to meet the demands of growth of
the Village Market and perform my day job. I also shared with
them my reluctance to ask for help when I knew they were
already doing so much.

Without hesitation, two things happened: First, they
each fussed at me for not delegating and for not trusting
them, the very people I had in place to be there for me as
they said they would. They assured me that they knew how

to advocate for themselves if they were overwhelmed—frankly, they'd just tell me. The second thing that happened: They leaped into action to take things off my plate. In so many different ways. Nadia and Carol picked up work orders. Courtney and Danyel worked with contractors. Kris made sure the front door ran smoothly during the events. I've never felt more supported than I did in those moments of complete vulnerability. What I learned about a village—about an authentic community—is that people want to support people and missions they believe in.

Importantly, *this two-way support is not quid pro quo.* You shouldn't be keeping score ("I helped Michelle last week, so she has to help me this week"). Not only is it tough to maintain relationships this way—purely transactional relationships don't allow for as much genuine connection and growth—but not everyone will have the skill set or resources to support you in the way you need at that given time. Everyone's resources are not the same, and in life sometimes we do more giving and sometimes we do more receiving. The goal is awareness. If it's your season to receive more, be committed to the time when you can begin to give more and do so.

I realize that sending out an SOS can be tough because it may feel like admitting weakness, and it requires overcoming pride, a fear of judgment, and more importantly, the risk of being let down. But trust the village that you are building and the people that you're attracting. If it's hard to ask for help, be honest—tell your people that you struggle with this. Being transparent allows them to show up for you in ways you really need. And asking for help allows you to gain new perspectives, learn from others' experiences, and solve problems more effectively.

If you are a convener, like me, create an opportunity to get people together who may struggle asking for help (it's not just leaders who are resistant to raising a hand!). For one of the Village Market's ecosystem-building events, we created an "All Hands on Deck" session for our entrepreneurs. All Hands on Deck is like speed-dating meets musical chairs, and it puts asking for help and sharing talent on blast. I put on a playlist and participants sit down with one other person to share needs and resources for the duration of one song. This encourages folks to be transparent in their asks, brag about what they are good at, and share trusted resources, whether it's public relations or tax advice or design. Tiana needs branding help? Maya happens to be great at branding. Serenity is looking for some legal assistance to incorporate? Thandie knows just the person. When the song stops, they move to the next table. There's a lot of laughing and learning and a "we're in this together" vibe. It eliminates a feeling of hierarchy and makes the village a true 360-degree circle of support, where everyone shows up fully for everyone else.

3. **Be inclusive.** I mean *truly* inclusive. The Black Lives Matter movement, which gained steam after the murder of George Floyd, shone a blinding light on the need for inclusion and equity, and it compelled corporations to address the enormous disparities in hiring, representation, and opportunity. While some progress was made, many racist groups are fighting against it. I've watched as funding and good-faith efforts have dried up over the last couple of years. There has been a backlash. Companies have slashed budgets for diversity, equity, inclusion, and belonging, and various public figures and institutions have decried the movement as a failure, even twisting it by asserting that reverse discrimination is at play. The reality: The work of inclusion and equity still needs to be done, period. There is zero doubt about that when you look at the data. Not only do vast racial and gender disparities

still exist, but research shows that closing the gaps is good for business: Diverse workforces are twice as likely to meet their financial goals compared to nondiverse workforces, and those that are intentionally inclusive in recruiting, hiring, promotion, and leadership report up to 30 percent higher revenue.

Whatever is happening in the corner offices of corporate America or the chambers of Congress or the courtrooms, I have control only over my business, and in my village we go beyond virtue signaling. I am consistently trying to practice diversity in all areas: race, age, economic and educational background, religious background, and LGBTQ+ representation. I intentionally incorporate diversity into my recruiting and hiring efforts when I select board seats for my nonprofit and choose entrepreneurs to partner with. My HR manager, who is wonderful at instituting impactful inclusion policies, also holds virtual diversity and anti-bias training regularly to ensure we maintain an inclusive environment.

As a company grows, it needs to continue learning. I recently hired a woman who is Muslim—my first employee (that I know of) who practices Islam—and she emailed me about taking time off for Eid al-Fitr, the feast day that breaks the fast of the holy month of Ramadan. I immediately responded that of course she could and reminded her that her personal days are for her to use however she needs. At that moment, I knew I needed to learn more; although I was already aware of Ramadan, I was not aware of Eid. What I did not do was ask my employee what the holiday was, thus placing the responsibility on her to educate me about it. Instead, I did my own research and set a meeting with my HR manager to ensure that our language was inclusive and mindful of different religious practices.

I encourage you to think deeply about the practices for your company and how you can be more inclusive. Be reflective, listen, learn, and evolve. The more people feel safe and seen by you, the more they will feel connected and respected and want to give to the workplace environment. In large corporations, I have often heard that it's hard to adjust the culture to significant needed changes. I often wonder if "hard" is just an excuse corporations give for not listening and practicing cultural sensitivity. My friends have told me stories of how they felt at work when George Floyd was murdered, recalling the silence, the avoidance to acknowledge that pain was present, the insensitivity to request that they have their Zoom cameras on, and the requirement to be bright-eyed and bushy-tailed and productive. I've asked them what they needed at that time—and during any instance of personal or collective grieving—and they stated thoughtful acknowledgment that sometimes the climate of the world seeps into work and that it's OK to not be OK and to take the time needed.

One form of diversity that isn't often discussed is age. Now, each generation is shaped by unique national events and cultural and political movements and thus brings a diversity of thought to a village. The worldview and communication style of a millennial—who came of age with the internet and 9/11—will naturally be somewhat different from those of a boomer or traditionalist (aka the silent generation), who experienced the civil rights movement and got their news from the radio or TV. But both can learn so much from each other. The resiliency of older generations, who have been through decades of ups and downs and are able to see moments as moments, offer perspective for younger generations who may feel the present will last a lifetime. (This is one reason elders make excellent observers and

enthusiasts.) The boldness and quick responsiveness of
millennials and Gen Z-ers, who were raised with a belief
in their own agency and for whom digital solutions come
quickly, model new and innovative ways to solve problems.
(As an older millennial, it's natural for me to ask questions,
to challenge—respectfully—what is presented.) During the
application process for the businesses we serve and the hiring
process for my companies, we are intentional about working
intergenerationally. We also adapt our practices for a range of
styles of communication—a mix of short-form SMS, long-form
e-mail, and Messenger; and virtual and in-person meetings.
The educator in me is always thinking about the unique
learning and communication styles people bring to the party
and how to get the message out in a variety of ways. I also
adjust my expectations based on the age and stage of my team
members. I don't expect that millennials or Gen Z-ers will be
with the organization for a decade; I understand that we are
raised in a more fluid job market than our parents, who may
have spent their entire working lives at the same company.
At Our Village United, we recently hired our first Gen X-er.
The younger team members were immediately in awe of her
effectiveness, wisdom, and resolve, and my Gen X-er loves
that the younger staff naturally think about automation and
technology first, which simplifies processes.

Diversity of thought also falls under the value of inclusion.
As I've said before, a community is not groupthink—that's
a cult. A strong community benefits from open discussions
about different approaches. A village should strive to be the
safest place to think and to evolve and to question your and
others' assumptions. Our monthly team-sharing sessions
provide a forum for all team members to share their successes,
concerns, and suggestions for solutions. Because everyone has
an opportunity to do this, there is no hierarchy in opinions

or a precedent set that one person's solutions matter most. I require only that the idea and potential solution be well thought out before presenting. It's been incredible to witness how the naturally quiet people feel empowered to speak up and share their important observations without fear of losing their job or some kind of retribution. And I've learned so much from the assistants, who are dedicated to their work but typically have grown accustomed to listening to supervisors and managers.

4.  **Be open to constructive feedback. Then reflect.** You cannot evolve if you are not willing to look at what isn't working and what your weaknesses are. Likewise, you cannot know what isn't working if you aren't listening to those you are in relationship with. This takes some agility, for you must remain soft and open while simultaneously cultivating a strong belief in your purpose and ability to lead.

    "Feedback" doesn't mean people just flat-out telling you you're wrong and for you to do exactly whatever it is they're telling you to do. That's not helpful, that's just being bossy. What I'm talking about is feedback offered with thoughtfulness and concern that suggests more inclusive or innovative ways of doing things. I tell my mentees to listen for that "ding" in the brain that lets you know when someone is offering genuine evaluation (again, this is why it's so important to do the work of being self-aware, so you can trust your internal compass). There's a feeling of safety and disarming that happens when you know you are being guided by someone who wants only the best for you.

    One way that I practice this value is through the servant style of leadership, which requires a great deal of feedback and reflection. Of all the leadership styles I've learned about, this one is the closest to how I believe a

community-first futurist should build, and it's helped me
use feedback to improve my team members' experiences.
Servant leaders care about their team and consider their
needs and assessments when making decisions; they
understand that prioritizing these relationships serves the
group mission. Servant leadership follows a set of principles
that includes *listening, empathy, awareness,* and *healing.* To
truly *listen,* I must employ compassion and *empathy*—putting
myself in someone else's shoes—so that I don't react with
defensiveness or dismissiveness when an employee says, for
example, that I'm too blunt for her comfort. If I react angrily
or unsympathetically, I erode their trust in me as someone
they can talk to. For me to have an *awareness* of which areas
to reform and *heal,* I must provide safe opportunities for
employees to communicate what is and isn't working for them.
It is important for leaders to provide moments for hands to
be raised, tough questions to be asked, and differing opinions
to be shared. My staff also know—for I have told them—that
they do not need to sugarcoat things or protect my heart or
worry about their job status by sharing. I tell them, "Part of
my job as the CEO is to take care of you."

But it can be challenging for team members to know when
or how to express misgivings. Done at the wrong time, it can
come across as defensive. Said in the wrong way, it can read as
disrespectful. One strategy that we've found helpful is having
one-on-one listening sessions with each employee so there is
a dedicated process for communication. They know that these
quarterly meetings are not about their work performance—I
simply ask questions about their experience, what they need,
what job security looks like to them, and examples of times
they've felt misunderstood. I also ask them to share what they
need from me as a leader. When a new employee has their
first listening session, they start out a bit reticent. But they

warm up when they see there is only one agenda: for them to
share anything and everything, without fear of judgment. I
may disagree with what I hear—and with certain employees
I have to brace myself because I *know* I won't hear a single
positive thing—but I sit with these uncomfortable moments
because they are essential to leading with a commitment to
the village.

When I am receiving feedback, I consider whether I've
heard it before (if so, it tells me it's likely a recurring truth)
and how this knowledge can help me achieve my expected
outcomes. I learned from one individual that I need to be
more vocal about letting her know what she is doing well, that
she could hear ten great things but that one negative thing
would send her reeling. I've also heard that team members
wanted more time with me (which made me happy!) in order
to build our relationships.

As I was growing the Our Village United team, I learned
from several members that they desired greater work benefits
to feel secure in their jobs. In the first year of the nonprofit,
because we could not afford health benefits, we instead
provided health-care reimbursement at a capped amount.
One employee confided that she viewed health insurance
benefits, understandably, as something she needed in order
to feel valued and to grow with the organization. It was a big
ask because our budget was tight, but it was also something
that I knew would help sustain my team and recruit more
great talent. I didn't make excuses—I told her I would make
it happen and announced to the team that health benefits
was a concrete goal. Would it take a while? Yes. But it was
worth doing. I believe in taking employees with me on these
journeys so they can see I take their concerns seriously. In
return, they hyped me up as I knocked down the deadlines
toward the goal. It took three years to raise the money, but at

the end of 2023 I was elated to be able to offer not only health benefits but a flexible work schedule, extended paid holiday breaks, and retirement benefits too. I was prouder than I've ever been receiving any award or public accolade. This is what success is to me—the ability to give my team something that would improve their lives, support their overall livelihood, and benefit their loved ones and the next generation as well. Leadership can't always deliver on every ask, but when your team sees you taking action, it encourages them to trust you as a leader and speak up more. It creates a culture of safety, inclusion, belonging, and overall trust. It's the essence of a village environment.

When I'm the one delivering constructive feedback, I do so with empathy and delicacy. I believe in being honest and kind, and in starting with the good. I acknowledge the work that a person has put into a project—even if it doesn't hit the mark, their effort deserves to be valued—and try to steer them in a better direction, asking, "Have you considered this other way of doing it?" and "What if we did this to take it from good to great?" If I have to deliver a no, I place myself in the position of the person on the receiving end. Is my tone empathic? Am I offering them hope for future success even though at this moment I am holding up a stop sign? I believe people in places of leadership have the responsibility to operate with a high level of emotional intelligence.

5. **Stay open. Stay patient. And know when to take the meeting.**
I cannot tell you how many times I have dragged myself to yet another meeting over coffee or squeezed a Zoom conference call into an already crowded day to engage a potential strategic partner. I do this because you never know how a connection will play out—this person may be the first in a series of three degrees of separation to meet that one

individual who is going to help change the trajectory of your business, who is going to be the domino that makes the others fall. I believe that the *community is always advocating on our behalf, even in the long periods of stillness when it feels like nothing is happening.* There are like-minded villagers behind closed doors you haven't yet knocked on, waiting for alignment to kick in. I trust assignment after assignment, because I have faith that allies are moving, quietly and unseen, in ways that will eventually bear fruit. I have many examples of this, but one in particular beautifully illustrates the importance of taking the call and that people are working on your behalf, often unbeknownst to you, when your purposes align.

In 2022, I was deep into my efforts to expand the work of Our Village United. In the years since the Honey Bubble kickoff in 2016, I had made progress in pursuit of my visions for the foundation—strengthening our programmatic offerings and applying for grants to help Atlanta-area solopreneurs flourish. But I had visions (those spiritual downloads) of doing more: growing the work nationally, including into Mississippi, my birth state; creating a national small-business tour that featured a pitch contest for businesses in our ELEVATE program; and awarding seed grants for first-time entrepreneurs. My dream was to partner with an established corporate giant that could springboard the work into the next phase. One afternoon, sitting at my laptop at my home office, I received an email from a wonderful woman at Mastercard named Rebecca with whom I'd already had many strategy meetings about the value of Our Village United partnering with Mastercard to expand my ELEVATE program. Between Rebecca and her colleague Stephen, we'd had countless conversations with various people at the company about how to move forward. Now Rebecca was asking me to take yet another meeting with yet another person at the company, Salah Goss, a senior vice president, who was in a separate division. My inner voice protested: "No, you are not doing another meeting. You don't have time for another conversation that won't lead anywhere." But because I am a "one more time" person who cannot live with the what-ifs—I need the peace and certainty that comes from having tried—I said, "OK." I swore this would be the last meeting I'd take with them.

Later that week, I met with Salah at the Village Retail, my store that's curated to showcase and sell products from Black brands, including some that participated in the programs offered at Our Village United. I wanted her to see the full circle of what we'd built for entrepreneurs . . . with limited funding. She, being a Black woman herself, understood the barriers our community was facing, and as a business-savvy funder, she saw that we had been measuring our data and could show results. She was impressed with my model and that we had paired education with commerce. I allowed myself to think, once again, "Maybe this is the person and the moment that unlocks the dream."

She was.

It was.

Three months later, we had a grant of $500,000 to launch the program nationally. I was flooded with gratitude. As I reflected on how it all unfolded, I once again recognized the truth that had shone forth throughout the years in my work and personal life: Community is always advocating for you, and even when you feel you are alone, there is a larger village that surrounds you. The quiet lulls are not always indicative of inactivity but rather of other people in the village on assignment, doing their thing, so that liftoff can eventually occur. *Your* assignment is to continue on your path, your purpose, with the belief and knowledge that there are pockets of community out there that will merge with yours when the timing is right. It took meeting with this particular person, after months of attempts, to make it happen. What I didn't know was that Rebecca and Stephen hadn't forgotten about me. They were still operating in their assignments on my behalf, trying different contacts at Mastercard until they had an aha moment with Salah.

Fast-forward to today: We have a full suite of business programming (five unique programs, mentoring, and wellness offerings) year-round and support more than four hundred entrepreneurs across the country annually. We have deployed more than $700,000 in grants and completed our first seven-city, national small-business tour in partnership with Mastercard in Solidarity and the BeyGood Foundation. We have worked with a number of other credible partners, including the Rockefeller Foundation, W. K. Kellogg Foundation, Wells Fargo, Target, Walmart, Clorox, the Jordan Brand, the White House Office of Public Engagement, and more. I have traveled across the country and outside the country to talk about our innovative village-led approach and why wellness serves as our foundation for our great work (I write about the undervalued role of wellness in chapter 6). We have dedicated office and work space in partnership with Pittsburgh Yards (an Atlanta community hub and coworking space) and the Annie E. Casey Foundation, where we serve as the programming partner for tenants in the building and the surrounding community. From an acorn, an oak tree has grown.

One caveat: Staying open and taking the meeting still means that you need to keep your values—and purpose—clear. Before I take meetings, I write down my intentions. I envision how I want it to go. I do my research on how we are aligned and how we can collaborate. I intently listen and stay fully present. (And when meetings conclude, I always

follow up in an email with a thank-you.) I've been guided
by trusting my internal compass, by having boundaries that
I won't compromise and deeply considered standards—
the ones you're reading through now—for how I run my
business. When something does not work out for me, I
practice reflecting, learning the lesson, and moving forward.
I allow myself space to remain open to new possibilities and
believe that something greater is working for me and for
the community. This has taken years of dedicated practice
of mindfulness and a belief that setbacks offer me greater
opportunities if I make the effort to learn from them.

6.  **The doing matters.** Only through intentional action do things
    shift in tangible ways and people experience a different life.
    It is in *the doing* that the change happens. It is in the doing
    where people learn to trust you as a leader—or frankly, in any
    role. People cannot live on hope talk alone—they must see the
    concrete things that are happening in order to develop a deep
    trust in working together. In order for people to desire more,
    they need to see something desirable, something that stirs
    their soul and gives them the drive to pursue something more
    or different. Marian Wright Edelman said, "You can't be what
    you can't see." Doing makes seeing possible.

    I am so convinced of this that I have made it my business's
    call to action. You'll see *Support Is a Verb* displayed in neon
    lights at every market, at the retail store, and on the merch we
    sell. Above all, the village is about doing. It isn't about creating
    symbols, it's about action. If businesses are struggling with
    accounting and legal services, then we create resources for
    knowledge-sharing and bridge relationships. We bring a master
    teacher in to teach or consult. We hire technical-assistant
    providers to offer pro bono services. If businesses need a
    retail store, the retail store is created. My purpose is tied to

actionable change because our community desperately needs things to shift. The doing doesn't only have to be big and bold to be meaningful. The unseen and minor acts matter just as much. In fact, there is great power in the small, intentional change. All of my enterprises are a testament to the power of a small, intentional village made of people whose purposes align and who are devoted to verbs. It can be hard to know which actions will have the most impact for your mission and when to move from ideation to doing. In chapter 8, I share the village verbs and action mindset that light up the path as we climb.

Village values are our guiding light. They keep us grounded and focused on the heart of the mission and the why. When you build in and for the community—as an entrepreneur, as a leader—values will help you navigate the not-so-good days, when the hard stuff bubbles to the surface.

## Reflection Questions

* What values do you have in place as you build your community and business?

* When you consider what might be missing from your business and community, who else can you share space with to fill a gap? Are there other futurists with skills you don't possess who could help springboard your dreams into reality?

* What practices are you building within your business and company to ensure you are inclusive and building thoughtfully?

* As you consider your next big decision for your business, ask yourself, "Who am I excluding?" If the answer is "no one," move forward. If there is some person or group you've neglected, how can you include them?

* Who have you connected with in the past whose mission is still on your mind, and are you considering them when opportunities cross your path?

* What processes do team members or clients have to share feedback on challenges and improvements?

* What actions can you tie to your goals?

* Other than the six values discussed in this chapter, what values speak most to you that you want to weave into your mission?

# FIVE

# Managing the Hard Stuff

MY FIRST TEACHING JOB OUT OF COLLEGE WAS AS AN ENGLISH teacher at Palmer High School, and working with my students was medicine to my soul. I was in my element as an enthusiast and a builder—I was helping them build their foundation so they could go out into the world and pursue their dreams. I would tell them, "If you leave here and you only learned things about English, I have failed you." When I closed my classroom door, we escaped the gruesome chokehold that the South can have on you, a region where the legacy of slavery, Jim Crow, and white supremacy still exists in the form of high rates of poverty, mass incarceration, low wages or unemployment, and barriers to health care. In our classroom, the students were freed from whatever home problems they were experiencing. I created a safe space to help them overcome the insecurities that arise during the teenage years—like a special little village inside the school.

When I made it to my fifth year of teaching, my classroom became a place of protection for me too. There had been changes at the school, and I felt at odds with some other people there, and then I heard some really cruel rumors floating around about me. None of them were true, but my reputation as a well-loved and celebrated teacher began to suffer. At the time, I couldn't understand what I did to make myself a target—my mom, whom I confided in, believed it all came down to jealousy. I'd walk down the hall and other staff members would get quiet. Even though it bothered me, I'd keep my head high and walk on. But that didn't make things any easier. My students shared with me that even they had heard disparaging things about me. This floored me, but I wouldn't allow the conversation to go further. Though I was young, I knew enough not to cross unprofessional boundaries with my students. I'd tell them, "If it's not about Toni Morrison or Phillis Wheatley, it is not allowed." They'd laugh and I'd chuckle. But internally, the microaggressions, the shunning, and the malicious gossip shook my spirit. My favorite place in the world, Palmer, felt less and less like a safe space. My principal—who was a good leader and kind person—listened to my complaints and tried to get things under control, but I had lost the joy I once felt at Palmer.

With firm love and guidance from my mother, who always tried to protect my heart, I accepted that it was time to leave. She wisely told me that the surest sign a relationship has surpassed its time is when it consistently takes more than it gives. She also told me that someone else's jealousy has nothing to do with me, and with love and honesty she saw that she needed to push me out of the nest. "Keysha," she said, "I know that you love your students, but there is something else for you. Something bigger than Palmer, and all of this is happening because it's time for you to move on. I don't know who you are gonna be, but you're supposed to be doing something else . . . something big, something special." She was right. The discomfort I felt at Palmer was so great that I could not stay. My enthusiasm for teaching was still there, but I no longer had passion for the environment of Palmer. I had to accept that my purpose there was done. I didn't want to leave the students, but I had to trust that someone else whose assignment was to teach would step in and do extraordinarily. I was ready for a new assignment and role in a place where I could blossom.

Though I left with internal scrapes and bruises, I carried with me many valuable lessons. Good things can come from tough moments. I had to mature my inner child, who always wanted to be in everyone's good graces. I had to understand that others' opinions and projections had nothing to do with me. My only responsibility was to live and behave honorably and to stay rooted in my principles. I discovered that community can change when people change and the culture shifts. It is fluid and evolving, and not always in a direction that is good for you. If you have no control over an environment, if you have a limited support system, and if it's harder and harder to source peace and joy, it's likely time to move on and embrace the next chapter. I also discovered that leaving what had become a toxic work environment opened up space for something better to come along, a place where my highest self could evolve. I continued to listen to what sparked me and followed that feeling. I opened myself up to new assignments—the teacher position at Calloway in Jackson and at South Cobb in Austell, Georgia, and my job at GADOE—discovering that I could fulfill my purpose in other communities and ultimately that I could build a community myself. If I had not left Palmer, I may not have made the move to Atlanta, met my coffeeshop entrepreneurs, and created the Village Market.

Not all difficult situations are this dire and require that you press the eject button. I am the type of stubborn learner who sometimes needs to experience an extreme amount of discomfort before I realize, "This isn't working any longer. It's time to go so I can grow." (I have gotten much better at tuning in to whether I'm truly happy and knowing when it's time to jump out of a burning building. Hint: If the building is on fire . . . probably time to exit.) Not every instance of discomfort is a sign you must close out one assignment to begin another or leave one community and start from scratch. Discomfort sometimes serves as an alarm bell that there's a pain point in your village that requires healing. Sometimes the tough moments are a product of societal and systemic barriers, and the thing to do is double down, to lean hard into your trusted community and purpose. Sustained discomfort can also be a sign that a change is needed within yourself. The challenge lies in discerning what is needed in that moment. What is the path for repair in the village? Should you continue to weather the discomfort for the greater good of the community? Have you tried absolutely everything and the assignment is to simply be patient, to allow community to show up in its own time and continue the progress? Or is the universe letting you know that you have reached your end point with a partnership, that you should part ways and give thanks for what you gave to it and what it gave to you?

There is also a danger in becoming too comfortable and stagnant. In order to grow we must be able and willing to experience some stress, some growing pains, to put ourselves in new situations. Sometimes we stay because it's easy and familiar. Now, if you're happy, there is absolutely nothing wrong with that. But there's a difference between being happy and being comfortable. Being comfortable or, worse, lackadaisical, is a passive state that doesn't offer potential for true growth. Ease without purpose doesn't bring you closer to fulfilling assignments or finding the *most* joy possible within your days. I've certainly been in situations where I stayed too long in a place because it felt like the safe thing to do, but over time I've become more confident with taking risks. We must learn to trust that we have the ability to handle a certain level of challenge in order to achieve our goals and visions.

Our culture tends to celebrate achievements rather than dwell on the tough moments—moments when the bank told us no, a manager let us go, or a customer left a bad review. But I believe there is responsibility in any village for those who have succeeded to share the hard moments to benefit those who come after them—to educate and lift as you climb. Otherwise, we cannot give an accurate sense of what to expect. This communal responsibility to lift as you climb is rooted in Black American history and helped ensure our safety and survival. During Jim Crow, many Black southerners fled to cities in the North to escape racial violence and pursue economic opportunities, known as the Great Migration. Families often put their money into one or two members to set them up in the North, and once transplants were on their feet, they would bring other family members to join them or send money to help those who chose to stay in the South. This happened in my family: My paternal grandfather moved to Chicago because there was no work in Mississippi—it's why many of my cousins were raised in the North. Every month he sent money to my grandmother to help support the family. My grandmother chose to stay in the South, and she is largely the reason I grew up in Mississippi. I view knowledge sharing in the same community light—a responsibility to reach back while also paving the way forward. When the next generation is better equipped, the path to liberation is a little bit clearer and safer.

Along with tears of joy and gratitude, I have experienced moments that stretched me, when I had to tell myself, "You will not break." There have been people along the way who couldn't understand my business concept or didn't have faith that it was substantial. The nos have the capacity to knock the air out of you. But the nos are a part of the journey, and if you can think of the rejections as redirections, there is an opportunity to learn from them. Believe me, nobody likes hearing no! But redirections afford you the ability to step back, refine your plans, and see that something was simply misaligned.

## IN THE FACE OF REJECTION, KEEP PUSHING . . . THEN SURRENDER

In the summer of 2019, three years after I'd launched the Village Market, I felt stuck. I wanted to meet the growing demands of vendors and foot traffic, and so I'd been trying for months to get sponsors. But it just wasn't happening, and I did not want to place the financial burden of expansion on our participating businesses or the villagers who came out to shop by increasing their fees. Finding sponsors was the best solution, but I had no idea how to go about securing them. I'd been going to meeting after meeting, making a strong case to corporations and local companies to back us, enthusiastically and painstakingly laying out the path for success that I believed was possible. Still, I was getting nowhere—and it was draining me.

One day, I made my way to my car after a series of rejection meetings, practically limping under the weight of the stress and the exhaustion. I eased myself into the seat, leaned my head on the headrest, and said out loud, "I surrender." Tears started rolling down my face, which completely surprised me. I cry when good things happen to strangers and people I love. I cry watching *every* rom-com or coming-of-age movie but rarely due to stress of running the business. I usually just push through to find a solution, too stubborn to allow it to trigger my emotions. But on this day, I was spent. I felt devalued and unseen as I had to continuously explain the dire need to champion vastly underrepresented and underresourced Black businesses, even in the Black mecca of Atlanta. I felt triggered by the suggestions from would-be sponsors that buying Black was simply a trend. I was fatigued by having to explain why I did not want to hire a celebrity to amplify the Village Market, that I'd rather allow the community to drive the mission. My head throbbed as I replayed a comment from a colleague: "You'd have a higher value proposition if you lowered your standards some." All the months of trying played back in my head like a gif on loop. "I'm not putting myself through this anymore," I told myself. Rejection after rejection made me question if the Village Market could scale to the level I saw in my mind, even though I *knew* the quality of the experience had made an impact in my community and there was opportunity to grow more. I looked at my red, tired eyes in the rearview mirror, exhaled slowly, and simply surrendered. I had taken it as far as I could within my own ability. I accepted that there was nothing more I could do, that a power higher than me would have to step in in order for the ground to give way.

Our society praises "powering through"—and often that is what is called for—but there are times when the healthiest choice is to surrender. I've found that making that decision requires the ability to discern between *determination* and *forcing the issue*. My determination has gotten me far. Determination is doing everything within your power and with your committed community to solve a problem. With determination, you and your village will experience small gains, little nods from the universe that you are in alignment. So you keep going as far as that determination allows you to. Forcing the issue is when you have left no stone unturned and are still unable to move forward. There are no small wins, no nods; it's just you banging your head against the wall and getting bruised. When I hit an immovable wall after having tried my absolute best, I actively surrender. It's not giving up; it's a giving over. Surrendering moves me into a place of handing it over to the universe, to a higher power, which I believe takes over to carry you where you and the community are meant to be.

A few days after I surrendered, a stunning thing happened. A miraculous thing. Berto, my partnership lead at the time, called me excitedly to let me know that he had a wonderful call with representatives from the Ford Local Dealer who wanted a meeting. After that, good karma continued to flow in. I began to get calls and emails. "Hello, Dr. Key, I heard about your venture and would love to figure out how to work together." "Lakeysha, I was speaking to X and she mentioned you were looking for partners. I am interested in scoping out possibilities." The invites trickled in, and interest continued to grow. All the outreach I'd done for the past several months started to materialize. The validation I felt was immense. As much as I believe in my business, to have someone else say, "I have never experienced anything like the Village Market," is medicinal. I do not believe it was a coincidence that the moment I surrendered and acknowledged I had done my utmost was when things began to happen, when the seeds I'd planted sprouted. There is power in surrendering. There is power in acknowledging that you've committed ten thousand hours and have done all that you can do (putting in the work is essential).[*] The village has a miraculous way of showing up, seemingly right on time. For me, surrendering is a spiritual act, one that can be accompanied by pain and tears but which ultimately reveals a new horizon.

When you have thrown everything at it and are still facing inertia, it's a sign to stop, zoom out, and consider whether you should pivot or to simply be still. For me, stillness grants clarity and allows me to revisit the questions that I often ask myself when my vision gets blurry: Why am I doing this and what do I hope to achieve? How do I feel? In those answers, I can see my next steps.

## SHIFT FROM SCARCITY TO ABUNDANCE

A vision of shared prosperity is a mindset of abundance. Abundance is an outlook that is in direct opposition to scarcity, which holds that resources are limited and there aren't enough to go around. (Economists define "abundance" more specifically as unlimited resources that are free from demands and needs.) Scarcity is not only a mindset but a tool—and a very effective one when used to sow division

---

[*] The ten-thousand-hours rule was introduced by one of my favorite writers and thinkers, Malcolm Gladwell, in his book *Outliers*. He deduced, based on research, that to become a master at a complex skill—even if you have innate talent—it takes a laser-focused commitment of around ten thousand hours of dedicated time.

and disenfranchise already marginalized groups. The concept of scarcity makes people think that there isn't enough—housing, funding, opportunities—so they become divided in efforts to secure what little they believe (or are made to believe) is available. I've certainly felt that panic when I first started to experience turnover in my staff. I had to shift my mindset. Initially, I worried that it would be hard to replace top talent, but now I give gratitude for the time spent and become excited about what a new team member will bring.

Fear and scarcity take people out of community because it sets up a me-versus-them dynamic instead of an all-of-us approach. It feeds a self-made mindset rather than a village mindset. It steers Black communities away from what we know works for our progress: available resources that are equally shared. Scarcity makes the hard stuff harder; it even invents the hard stuff. As Isabel Wilkerson writes in her book *Caste*, manufactured scarcity keeps people in a caste system—artificial societal divisions that limit people's opportunities and resources based on race. Scarcity causes folks to fight over little scraps of food because they are made to starve. It's meant to keep people hungry and underfed. It's meant to keep people divided because together they'd realize the true enemy and become powerful.

I grew up humbly, so when I say "abundance," I don't mean material riches. Though my parents worked incredibly hard and provided my siblings and me with all the essentials and the love we needed to thrive, we lived very humbly. Abundance for us was pizza on Fridays. Abundance was moving into a home whose roof no longer leaked when it rained and that had indoor plumbing. Abundance was also being able to imagine more than what you are shown, to believe in what may not seem possible to others but which is imminently possible in your mind's eye. Although I never felt scarcity growing up (I'm still impressed with how my parents shielded us), I didn't want my parents to have to work as hard as they did. I would sign my mom's birthday and Mother's Day cards "your future millionaire author and speaker" not only because I believed in a prosperous future for myself but also because I so desperately wanted to share the hopefulness and fullness of my beliefs with my mother. I knew one day I'd help my parents live a life of ease. I didn't know to call it a mindset of abundance at the time, but that's what it was. My beliefs were affirmations, enveloped in a headspace of enough.

When the pandemic hit in 2020, the world as we knew it changed. Hospitals were filling up; we were being advised to stay home. Schools closed. People were dying. When would it end? No one knew, not the mayor, not the president, not the Centers for Disease Control and Prevention (CDC). As a Black female entrepreneur, I was used to uncertainty, but this was unreal. I'd fielded my share of nos from humans, but this felt like the universe was saying no to everyone on the planet. I remember how terrifying it was each day during lockdown to wake up with no precedent for how to move forward. As the weeks ticked by, one thing did seem certain: I'd have to cancel my spring Village Market event. My business model was driven by large in-person events. How could we continue without IRL togetherness? In March, right after the NBA announced they had canceled their season, I called Sonovia, my right hand—a tireless collaborator and a keen observer—and said, "I think we've got to cancel." We were crushed. Our spring event was slated to be the largest marketplace to date, following closely on the heels of our 2019 Black Friday marketplace, which was a massive success. Our team had been on a high, and I felt that I had finally gotten past the toughest parts: We had sponsors. We had "street credit" from the businesses who had already participated—they spoke of the Village Market as a venture that truly cared about boosting their sales and enriching their experience as entrepreneurs. We had buy-in from the community, who were excited to support and spend on businesses they knew were pouring back into the village. Despite this momentum, I knew that closing the curtains was the only decision. Like most people, I was anxious about what COVID *was* exactly. I entertained doomsday thoughts, wondering, "This could be the 'last days' that my church-going grandmother randomly reminds me of—often." I was worried about both of my grandmothers, my dad and siblings, my friends and extended family. I wanted my business team to be safe. I was also increasingly worried about the financial security of the many Black businesses the Village Market supported. My email inbox was flooded with messages from entrepreneurs reaching out about their future and fates. I had the same worries about my own company. It looked as if the Village Market might be among the 52 percent of small US businesses that would ultimately shutter.

In the days after I pulled the plug on the in-person event, I grappled with the profound sadness of letting go of it and the uncertainty of my future; I wondered what I was supposed to do next. Who was I, at this moment, for my business, my community, and my family? I sat with the uncertainty. A feeling of fear—of scarcity—started creeping in. If things kept going in this direction, what would befall my beloved entrepreneur community? I knew that no matter whatever was happening with the pandemic, businesses owned by people of color would be the most impacted.

Despite the fear and sadness, I felt certain that my purpose had not changed. I was meant to lift up Black entrepreneurs in my community. And one thing I knew for sure was that I wasn't going to wait on anyone else to be a savior, I was simply going to do what I knew to do and felt called to do. I decided that I was going to try to save my company and help others stay open.

But how?

I made a decision, practically overnight, to replace the in-person spring marketplace with a digital version. We would not be canceling, we would not be driven by fear, we would reinvent ourselves. I knew in my heart this would be a onetime event—a digital marketplace was not an ongoing feature of my big-picture vision—but it was the only way to support our businesses during this unprecedented upheaval. I announced the decision to the vendors and public right away, before we had even nailed down the details: I hired an animator to develop a commercial to promote the market. The response? The community was thrilled. They had something promising and tangible to latch on to in the midst of uncertainty.

We had only three weeks to pull it all together. So the team—six people who'd been with me for several years and who trusted me and believed in the vision—got to work. We built an e-commerce site so the community could shop. We interfaced continually with vendors to make sure they had what they needed to become digital sellers. On the day of the digital market, thirty-eight thousand people participated in the experience. It was a success, and although it didn't reach the profitability level of past markets, it made a huge difference for the businesses that joined in.

Creating this virtual experience took everything out of us. It required us—Carol, Berto, Danyel, Sonovia, Nadia, Dameon—to work around the clock. During those weeks, it was not unusual to have seven-hour conference calls—yes, seven hours. Sleep was sporadic. We were exhausted and annoyed with one another, but we did it. I could not have overcome this huge hurdle (and the many more to come) without these particular people in place, villagers who had my back because I had theirs, whom I had been in community with for years, intentionally building strong and respectful relationships. And I could not have moved myself and the team out of a place of stagnation, in the midst of what felt like a never-ending storm coming from all corners, without a belief in abundance, without a belief that in the middle of chaos and uncertainty, we could thrive together.

## WHEN YOU HIT A WALL, PAUSE . . . THEN PIVOT

I wish I could say that the digital market secured the Village Market's future. It did not. It was a temporary bandage—albeit an important one—that kept us and others afloat for the time being. The pandemic was still raging and businesses were still hurting. What I did know: My team and I needed a break. So I took the time, when the world had slowed to a crawl, to step back. I encouraged my team to do the same and continued to pay them during this downtime so they could rest and not worry about finances. This forced pause gave me the opportunity to finally exhale, to breathe. It wasn't until I no longer had to do anything but exist at home in my oversized PJs on my couch, responsible for no one but myself, that I realized I had been operating in a state of near-constant stress. I felt relieved for the first time in years. I actually rested when I slept, instead of waking with a start at 3:00 a.m. When the CDC advised that it was safe to finally leave the house, I went for long walks and bike rides. I hiked all over Georgia—Cloudland Canyon State Park, Providence Canyon State Park (the state's "Little Grand Canyon"), and Sweetwater Creek State Park. I went on a cross-country road trip, discovering the many mountains and trails of Colorado and Utah and exploring the canyons and sand dunes of Nevada and Arizona. I talked to friends more. I laughed more and actually watched TV (*Queen Sugar* and *The Chi* were my favorites). I learned how to cook new foods and recipes by watching my friend Tabitha Brown's TikTok and Instagram.

As I built myself back up physically and mentally, I began to gain clarity surrounding the Village Market's future. I was starting to accept that saving my business would require more than just replicating what I'd done in the past. It appeared that the pandemic had no end in sight. Hospitals were still flooded; the country was in unrest due to the murder of George Floyd; people were at odds about the vaccine, and it was not clear what was next . . . for any of us.

I stopped considering the next Village Market event. For several days I allowed myself to grieve the ending of this chapter, what had been my life's work for almost five years. I had to let that story end so I could start a new one. I just had to figure out how to fill the next set of pages. Not once did I consider taking a job and working for someone else, though. I took solace and strength in the fact that when I considered my greater purpose, raising up Black entrepreneurs, I still experienced a profound peace. I began to understand that I would have to build something different and that whatever it was could be better and bigger and even more impactful. It would require me to pivot, and in a big way.

One important aspect of an abundance mindset is the pivot—the ability to swivel in a different direction when you hit an impasse. The end of one pathway does not mean the end of the business or the project. We don't always need plan A to work out. In fact, sometimes plan B or plan C offers a better solution. A pivot means you see another way to get to your destination other than the original route. A pivot is inherently optimistic, and when you do it with a committed team, you can do the hard things. Once I arrived at this decision, I felt the energy in me rise and the creative juices flow. I wrote about my pivot plan in my Notebook of Brilliant Ideas (yes, that's the name) and began with a list of questions:

* What is accessible to me? Which networks and platforms are available to me as a business owner?

* What am I still passionate about?

* What scares me some? (Anything that potentially intimidates me allows me to identify my blocks—anxiety, fear, impostor syndrome—process them and move past them.)

These reflections allowed me to center my "why"—building a viable village and financial prosperity for Black businesses—and I dreamed up ways to plot out the next story. I asked for clarity, and my visions started to form. What was taking shape in my mind was something that, at first glance, seemed ill-advised in a pandemic. A retail store. A brick-and-mortar space, open daily, to draw people together, indoors. I saw many Black businesses sharing a permanent and vibrant space, with customers happily milling about. Perhaps families stumbled on it as they were running errands and were drawn in by the beautiful products and positive vibes. Others might come because they'd heard about it and had made a dedicated trip to experience the store.

But my vision didn't stop there. I thought about who these entrepreneurs were—what were their stories? They were folks who had everything going for them—the intention, the drive, the excellent products—but they lacked opportunity and support. They were flourishing in the store because they had entered into a community where they were lifted up in every way—they had been nurtured and believed in and funded. They were folks who'd launched from an incubator flooded with grants and opportunities of every kind, a source of abundance. I was envisioning, hand in hand with the store, a nonprofit foundation, a matured version of the bubble tea shop entrepreneurs and their successors, class after class of graduates.

When I get to a loud, full-body yes, I am ready to go. There is an absence of fear and no second-guessing. My mind gets on board, the builder in me arrives, and I start to connect the dots and actualize the idea. You may not think you have visions, but you most certainly have ideas that continue to come to you. I believe those ideas are visions as well, even if you cannot fully see the clear picture.

So I began. I built out the model for a retail store, following my vision and posing key questions to help flesh it out. A good practice when you have an idea is to ask yourself what outcomes you'd like to experience and who is in your village to help you build. For me, I thought about a wonderful woman, Melita, I'd met through another friend, Allison, who had the great idea of putting together an intentional group of women. Melita was experienced in retail store design. My friend Dayle, who was also a part of the group, popped into my mind—she was gifted in brand products and merchandising. My sister Yolanda was an operations pro with over sixteen years of experience in that sector. I believe we are in close proximity to what we need when we are fulfilling our purpose. My community was forming.

Nothing inside me said, "Key, you haven't done this before." You may have heard of the growth mindset, the belief that you can grow your talents and be successful through learning, strategies, and input from others. The learning component here is essential, because it means that you recognize there are other possibilities to explore, additional knowledge you may not yet have that can open up new corridors. It assumes that even in the face of challenge, there is more out there—*enough* out there—for you to keep going, to keep risking. It assumes that other people on your team may see solutions that you do not and that embracing those ideas benefits the whole. It allows the pivot to be doable.

A growth mindset is the opposite of a fixed mindset; with the latter, you believe success is reliant on an innate talent that you either have or you don't, period—no learning possible. But believing that some people are just naturally successful and belong while others aren't and don't belong disempowers you. It steals your confidence, negates your hard work, and shuts down your progress. No one has mastered everything; no one is perfect all the time. Anyone who says otherwise is pretending (or they've unlocked the secrets of the universe)!

A growth mindset accepts that blunders and pivots are part of the journey and that as long as we are doing our best, committed to the challenge, and collaborating with others, we *do* belong. Of course, no one is meant to have a 100 percent growth mindset (experts say we are actually a mix of both mindsets—because yes, people do in fact have innate talents!), but companies that promote a growth mindset in their employees and organization report a work culture that is more collaborative and innovative and employees who are more committed and empowered.

Five months later, in November 2020, my team opened the flagship store of the Village Retail at Ponce City Market, which gets some of the highest foot traffic in the city. Five months is a ridiculously short runway to take flight, but we were determined to make it happen—and we had an incredible team bringing their skills and vision to the project. Melita, Dayle, and Yolanda brought their gifts and commitment to the assignment, resulting in a wondrous alignment. It also helped that there were fewer applicants for retail space during the pandemic and that the Black Lives Matters movement had awoken people to the need to support Black businesses. Today, we employ over a dozen team members and a host of contractors, helping to support thousands of Black businesses.

It's ironic, but some of the moments that enable you to overcome the toughest challenges for your community happen in isolation. I read that Dr. Martin Luther King Jr. practiced his speeches at home alone before he stepped in front of his audiences. He wanted to show up believable for his people when it was time to come together, so he used alone time to pray, listen, and practice. For me, the pandemic forced the pause that I needed to get clarity and successfully pivot. That experience taught me that I need to do this on a consistent basis. I believe that all leaders should regularly and proactively press pause. It pulls you out of the day-to-day details—the onslaught of emails and texts, the wall of meetings—so you can reflect on whether the goals you're working so hard for with your community truly line up with your vision and purpose. It's looking at the building from the outside and then taking a look inside to ensure the outside matches the inside, and vice versa. If a company is great for the customer, the environment internally should reflect that positive experience for the employees as well. The practice gives me clarity, and a clear and intentional mind is a powerful one.

My decision to pause and surrender to the new circumstances we were living under created new feathers in the Village Market's wings. That surrender ushered in the opportunity for reflection, new ideas, and new iterations of my company. Toni Morrison wrote in *Song of Solomon*: "If you surrendered to the air, you could *ride* it." When you stop going against the wind and allow it to take you, where you go will likely surprise you. The challenge is knowing when to press forward with your vision and when to allow the wind to carry you in a different direction.

## WHEN YOU GET IT WRONG, LEARN THE LESSON

Several years ago, the Village Market had a big opportunity to support a large conference for global professionals. Collaborating with conferences had been on my bucket list for years, so I excitedly said yes . . . but with some trepidation because of the fact that we had very little time to prepare for it. Nor was I able to speak directly with the primary cofounder, someone I'd only met once, prior to signing the contract. Still, the organizers promised that the kickoff conversation would happen after the ink was dry. It wasn't how I liked to do things, but this was a *huge* get, and on paper it really looked like our values aligned: professionals from around the world coming together to empower one another. Normally, I ask several important questions when I'm considering whether to enter into a partnership: What are your community values? How do you handle conflict? What is your team's preferred style of communication and your style of leadership? I believe it's critical to have these sometimes-uncomfortable conversations up front, especially when the project time frame is so incredibly tight—we were being asked to do in a few weeks what normally takes about a year. It would be a *very* heavy lift, but the ambitious side of me was elated by the opportunity. Would it be a challenge? Sure, but it was one I felt confident we could take on. I shared with my team that we would be working some long hours, that it would be tough, but they were also excited and all in.

The problems began soon after we signed the contract. The call I was supposed to have with the cofounders to raise those essential questions was canceled. Twice. There was no blueprint in place to follow. Clients of the conference were, understandably, already complaining about the lateness of everything. Between middle-of-the-night email rants and irritating daytime calls from folks on the leadership team, each interaction seemed to get steadily worse. I felt terrible that I had put my staff in the path of this hurricane, and I did my best to buffer them and keep their spirits up as we slogged through what I can only describe as weeks of hell. I was also increasingly distressed that my company was being blamed for everything that was going wrong, even though we'd been on the project for only a few short weeks. Our reputation was taking a hit with every day that passed. It was the opposite of how I like to do business—being prepared, prioritizing client needs, and staying positive in a supportive, collaborative environment.

The experience reached peak nightmare the day before the conference opened. I was on one side of the venue helping out a client when I received a phone call from one of my team members. "Doc, we need you over here, there's a volatile situation unfolding." I raced over to the other side of the venue to find two tall men—clients at the conference—towering over my employee, angrily expressing their frustrations. I told my team members that I would handle it. I didn't want them in the firing line. Suddenly, one of the clients started yelling as they approached me. We had to call security, who de-escalated the incident. They were allowed to stay (for appearances). I had to absorb the vitriol.

On the drive back to the hotel, I asked the driver to stop and let me out so I could walk—I felt my chest tightening and I needed air. I wasn't five steps out of the car when my chest started heaving up and down as I struggled to inhale. Then the tears fell. I was completely gutted. This was my tipping point. Weeks of compounded stress overtook me. I felt defeated and angry and very responsible for exposing my team to this whole toxic experience. While I truly believed in our ability to deliver, I had made a wrong decision, one that might very well have a negative lasting consequence on my company. I was so disappointed in myself for going against my inner knowing. I hadn't listened to the businesswoman voice inside me saying, "There's no way you can pull this all off well in that short time frame!" I was starry-eyed and eager for the opportunity to accomplish a dream goal, and I let my ambition take the wheel, overriding all the instincts and experience I had. I should have insisted on speaking with the founders to know their mindset and expectations as decision-makers *before* we sealed the deal. I also made an assumption that some standard operating procedures were already in place. In many ways I convinced myself that because we were mission aligned, we were also values aligned.

That night, I walked around for three hours, trying to calm and ground myself. I needed to return to leader mode and get everyone through the next several days, but I was embarrassed that it had reached this crisis point. I was honest with the team and confirmed for them that yes, things were as bad as they seemed. We were in partnership with a chaotic team that wasn't getting the structure or leadership they needed from above. I believe in calling a thing what it is, to not downplay the obvious harm or the microaggressions, which would be gaslighting. I then apologized and asked for their forgiveness. They were gracious enough to give it, even though I'm sure it wasn't easy for them.

Honestly, I had a much harder time forgiving myself. To this day, it is one of the worst decisions I've ever made in business. Months afterward, when I'd see emails from the conference team, my chest would tighten and I'd get sharp stomach pains. It took several weeks for me to stop waking in the middle of the night gasping for air. It took a few more weeks for the experience to escape my dream space. It took many sessions with my therapist to stop obsessing over it and wishing I could undo it all, to stop blaming myself for everything and ruminating over the mistakes we did make—where our missteps (due to the lack of understanding) contributed to the chaos. And it took time for me to rebuild confidence in myself and to recognize that while I wished things had gone differently, I had learned a lot from making this particular mistake.

What helped in making that turning point was to focus on the lessons. After the pain, I unpacked what I've learned. This practice is challenging to start, and I understand that. It involves reflecting on the most painful part of an experience and accepting that the experience cannot be changed. It's easy to turn this into an exercise in self-flagellation and get caught up in rumination over how you *feel* about what went wrong, but the point is to access and then move through the discomfort. If you don't absorb the teaching, your company cannot move forward, and neither will you. Trust me, I thought I'd already learned to check my ego and ambition at the door, to be driven only by purpose and my gut, to await my full-body yes. But this had shown me that I still had work to do on that front. It showed me that you can receive the things that you've wanted, but sometimes the test is to see if you can recognize that it isn't the best thing for you or your business. Will you say no to it and trust that the opportunity or another opportunity that is more realistic will come in time? In this case, of course, I wish I had, but obviously, that wasn't how the situation played out.

Here's what I learned.

Take responsibility. No one is free from mistakes. We weren't. Secondly, beginning a collaboration with an honest and open conversation about communication, realistic expectations, and values is critical. I believe that if the leadership team and I had spoken directly and transparently about the state of the conference and the timeline of the request, they might have been more supportive and also seen how committed and honored we were to work hard for them and their mission. They may have felt more inclined to respond from a place of collaborative problem-solving, not blaming or shaming. Maybe. And one of the biggest lessons I learned—and it's a good business practice—is not to take on things that are presently in chaos (aka cleanup jobs) unless you are Olivia Pope. The debris is bound to affect you too.

Recently, one of my team members suggested we do the conference again "to show them all," since we now knew the landscape. It was tempting, and we laughed about it, but I knew that I wouldn't move ahead. Sure, it would've been great to return and blow it out of the water, but that was just ego talking. It was out of alignment. I wasn't going to jeopardize my team, my values, my company, or my reputation again. I decided it was better to stay purposeful, mission driven, and forward thinking.

## WHEN YOU *KNOW* YOU'RE RIGHT, PERSEVERE

Following the murder of George Floyd in May 2020, when corporations started publicly caring about Black people and Black businesses, many Black-led organizations began to receive grant money in amounts heretofore unseen. My own nonprofit submitted a concept note—an outline submitted prior to the grant proposal process—for a Rockefeller Foundation grant worth $500,000. This would be the first grant award for Our Village United. We were pretty far into the process, and all indications pointed to a yes. If it came through, it would be a giant leap, a vision made real. My team and I scrupulously went through the process, making sure we had all our ducks in a row, including our 501(c)(3) paperwork, which allows the IRS to make a determination that you are, indeed, a nonprofit.

When I logged on to the IRS site to print out proof of our 501(c)(3) status, lo and behold, it said we'd lost our determination. I didn't panic; I thought, "Oh, it's just a mistake, I'll call the IRS and see what's going on." Now, I'm sure anyone who has had to deal directly with the IRS is laughing at my naivete. Apparently, you don't just get the IRS on the phone and everything is solved. No, it took days of nonstop calls to finally speak with a human who did not respond like a robot and still *more* days and more conversations to get an understanding of what was going on.

By this point, I *was* panicking. We were at real risk of losing our first grant, which I had earmarked to launch my ELEVATE program. If I didn't do anything, I was pretty sure that the grant would disappear. So I did what I knew to do: I reached out to someone who had the expertise I did not. I contacted a friend who was an attorney in Atlanta, and she referred me to a certain tax attorney who had worked at the IRS. I hired him immediately (and contacted a tax advocate, which the IRS provides), and he discovered that the IRS was claiming that we had not filed a 990 form (quick tutorial: a 990 provides detailed financial information to justify your tax-exempt status, and it's a *must*). I called the firm we'd hired to handle all our IRS paperwork, and they confirmed, "Yes, we did file this form. The IRS is wrong." The tax attorney wrote a letter to the IRS stating the error needed to be corrected ASAP, but the timeline for their ruling turned out to be . . . indefinite. *We did not have indefinite amounts of time. We had a matter of days.* As so often happens in life and in business, it was the best of times and the worst of times, all at once. Here I was on the precipice of being awarded my first grant ever—and in a huge amount—but I was in jeopardy of losing it because of a bureaucratic error that I, frankly, had no control over.

It seemed as if things were falling apart, but my certainty that we were in the right kept me locked in perseverance mode. We'd done everything we were supposed to do, so this was not a time to surrender. I knew in my heart that this was not a sign from the universe that I was on the wrong track or that I had to pivot. This was not me forcing the issue. Too much was riding on this—the future of my nonprofit was at stake. So I did the thing that I'd been dreading, something that caused me an extreme amount of discomfort: I had to call the Rockefeller Foundation—and every single one of the organizations we were in grant talks with, including Target and

AT&T—and ask for patience and their trust that this was an error on the IRS's part. It was incredibly embarrassing for me to have these conversations, having prepared as much as I did while also knowing that these were people I was just starting to build connections with. As I dialed each contact, my heart beat faster. I feared the worst, that they would think, "This is why we don't invest in Black-led organizations, they don't have their act together."

There was reason for me to feel this way too; the data back it up. Racially driven stereotypes and systemic racism have been working against Black nonprofits for decades. Organizations led by people of color have budgets that are 24 percent smaller than white-led organizations, in great part because of the lack of access to funding. White-led organizations largely grow, while Black-led organizations largely flounder, often unable to completely fulfill their communities' needs. Even knowing this, and the risk of making these calls . . . I still had to try. I knew I had the truth on my side.

The beautiful thing was that nearly every single person I spoke to responded with compassion and extended me that trust. They could have given ground to misgivings or prejudice or simply said, "Well, those are the rules, sorry." But they didn't. They heard my intention and my appeal for their understanding and they responded in kind. I can't imagine being more relieved than I was in those moments, seeing that while the relationships were still in the nascent stage, there was a tremendous amount of goodwill. I believe that sometimes we are granted compassion in tough situations so that we can practice empathy and understanding with others.

For the next few weeks, I was on pins and needles, constantly looking at my phone and waiting.

Then, finally, we got the final word that yes, we were going to receive our first grant award! I was *elated* and remember running around my house. The larger village had trusted me and believed in me because of the work I'd put in over the years, and because I'd persevered, it all worked out. Seven long months later, I received a letter from the IRS stating, "We erroneously placed you on our auto-revocation list," and that our 501(c)(3) determination was now reinstated. It felt sooooo good to send that letter to everyone who believed in me. Would it have been possible to get there without their support? Of course not. I couldn't have done this without determination and a well-resourced community that supported me in finding a tax attorney. Neither could I have done this without partners at each of the organizations who spoke up on my behalf, who believed in me and my organization's purpose.

## FIGHT INEQUITY WITH INTENTIONAL ACTION

I'll state the obvious: Inequality and inequities exist. They are what they are. They are performing efficiently and effectively, just as they were designed to do. They are tools meant to ensure that things are hard and often impossible for Black people and other people of color. Though inequities may not always be in the front seat, they are going to continue to be a passenger until inequality ceases to exist. You don't need me to list the statistics that bear this out, to tell you what you already have experienced—the delicate line that we walk knowing that the color of our skin can be stigmatizing and an invitation for bias and prejudice.

But here's where I want to shift the focus: As leaders of companies and organizations—as futurists and builders and collaborators—we have the fortunate power to do and build differently, to choose to give people, employees and clients, a different experience. This is what a twenty-first-century leader does. Only through intentional collaboration—with a village mindset and village values—can we progress in a meaningful way. One way to do that is through the values of group economics, something I explore in chapter 7. Changing entrenched constructs can be hard, but trust me when I say that each leader and each person can play a significant role by rewiring those constructs within their own company or organization.

While being in a leadership position in the Black community is a privilege, it also carries a level of responsibility that can feel heavy. I sometimes feel the weight of representing all Black companies and the burden of being excellent, with little to no room for public setbacks or failures. From listening to friends and interviews with successful Black entrepreneurs who have a social impact focus, I know they feel the pressure as well. And you don't have to be a leader to carry this burden. To counterbalance the weary load, I take regular solace in knowing that I am working to shift the landscape that makes this burden exist in the first place. And in doing so, I am helping create a new model that my family—and especially my young nephews—can look at and be encouraged by. After all, my business is grounded in helping Black people achieve successful businesses so more people and future generations can experience the bounty and prosperity. When I hired my sister to run my retail arm of the business, I brought her into my village not because we were related but because she had more than sixteen years of experience in that sector. She's talented, hardworking, and committed, and I knew she'd add incredible value to the team. She made us better. But despite being a Black woman who has achieved so much, she had been overlooked time and time again in her industry. She was not being seen. I saw her—not simply because she was my sister, but because of her expertise, how hard she worked, how passionate she was. She deserved a position and salary commensurate with her background and know-how. Wherever and whenever I have agency, I choose to see the value in what others overlook. We must see and hire each other. We can build and lead in ways that counter inequity and inequality. Just as my classroom was a refuge for students, a place of safety from the harsh realities of the outside world, my business provides relief from the burdens of inequality and opportunity for those who seek the same values. In order to weather ever-present inequality and challenges and to stay connected to purpose, I have learned that self-care is foundational. For me and every member of my village. Without it, neither you nor the community can show up as your best selves.

## Reflection Questions

* Has there ever been a time when you felt you were in the wrong village or a community that held no support or promise for you? Looking back, what was the moment that let you know it was time to exit, and what opened up for you when you left that community?

* What support system do you have in place to help you manage the hard stuff?

* How did you react the last time you faced a challenge? Is there anything you wish you would have done differently? What perspective would you bring into a similar situation if faced with it now?

* Think of a problem you are currently grappling with. What would it mean to view that issue through a mindset of abundance?

* Is there someone in your village who could benefit from hearing about a time when you stumbled and recovered? Is there someone you admire whom you can ask, "What is one of the hardest challenges you've faced, and how did you overcome it?"

* If you are facing something incredibly difficult right now, can you reflect to determine whether you should surrender and pivot or whether you are experiencing enough small wins to stay determined?

★ Consider a time someone approached you with a hard conversation. How did you respond? What felt good in that conversation, and what did not feel good?

★ What is your vision for how a community can manage hard times in healthier ways?

# SIX

# Self-Care and the Well Community

AFTER TWO YEARS OF PULLING DOUBLE DUTY—WORKING MY full-time job at GADOE and growing the Village Market—I reached an impasse. One evening, at the end of another very long day filled with meetings, employee trainings, and an endless list of to-dos, I caught a glimpse in the bathroom mirror and was startled by the woman looking back at me.

Who *was* that?

My eyes were red and strained. My skin had lost its natural glow and looked dull and lifeless. Seeing that, I was suddenly acutely aware of the body aches and chronic fatigue I had been trying to ignore for months. I'd started seeing a therapist to get a handle on my anxiety, but I still had a hard time catching my breath in moments of distress, and my brain wouldn't shut off, even when I hit the pillow, desperate for sleep. But it couldn't be *that* bad . . . or so I kept convincing myself.

I told myself that I could not rest. Not with my dreams of the Village Market coming to fruition. I had to stay in the momentum that was thrusting us forward, convinced that if I slowed down, it would all stop and my dreams would be deferred. So I went to my doctor, requesting that she run every lab test possible, hoping she'd find a nutrient deficiency I could solve by popping a daily supplement. I didn't, however, mention my recent onset of chest pains or that I had moments of shallow breathing. Now wasn't the time to get sidetracked . . . I had too many deadlines and big ideas that I had to fully see through.

A week later, I sat with my doctor to review the test results. There weren't any major concerns, thankfully, but as she asked about my lifestyle, she pointed out the obvious facts: I wasn't drinking enough water, I wasn't sleeping or eating well, I had low energy, and my stress was running rampant, exacerbating a previous diagnosis of irritable bowel syndrome. "If you do not listen to your body, it will make you listen," she gently warned me. I listened to the part I wanted to hear, that there was nothing *seriously* wrong. I told myself, "Yes, I can keep going." I drove to the first meeting of the day—the first of seven. My temples throbbed through every single one. When I finally made it back to my car, I closed my eyes to decompress and practice the breathing exercises that my friend Dr. Crystal Jones advised me to do. I played back the meetings in my head, and my heart sank as I had to concede that none had really led to the opportunities that I thought they would. This was the day of no.

No, *not at this time.*

No, *it's not a good fit.*

No, *we do not sponsor events like this.*

No, *sorry.*

I felt my breath getting shorter. Finally, all of those months of stress and anxiety that I'd left unaddressed were tumbling out. Tears fell because of the many months of three to four hours of sleep at night. Because of the intense stomach pain I experienced almost anytime I ate. Because I deeply missed my mother, who had recently transitioned, and depression was creeping back into my mental space.

Deep down, I knew my doctor was right. I had to make significant changes. I knew that in order for me to show up with the energy and optimism and empathy needed to lead my village, I had to return to my daily self-loving practices of taking care of myself. I had to take back my mind and fight for the person who was drowning, not only for myself but for my community as well.

Audre Lorde said it best: "Caring for myself is not self-indulgence, it is self-preservation, and that is an act of political warfare." Lorde understood the interconnectedness between the health of the individual and the health of the community, between a state of wellness and the power to make changes, to thrive holistically. Truly seeing one another requires rested eyes and a body that is not in conflict with its soul. To effectively build together requires a resolved spirit that is void of intimidation and envy. To get to this place, we must be dedicated to doing our personal soul work. To be catalysts for each other's greatness, we must show up in our own greatness, and we can only do that when the mind, body, and spirit are intact.

Think of it this way: If the gas tank in your car is empty, and a friend calls asking you for a ride, how are you going to help her when *you're* on empty? I believe that it's almost impossible to be truly present for someone else in the community when you are in grave need yourself. As psychologist (and my friend) Dr. Joy Beckwith often says, "You can't pour from an empty cup." We need futurists to be balanced in all aspects of their life—physically, emotionally, and spiritually—in order to lead the community with thoughtful, village-made values. We need villagers who are invigorated for their assignments and who create a community of care around themselves. When you are building differently, creating more equitable systems and pathways, you will receive pushback and meet roadblocks—even when you are in alignment. Having self-loving habits and practices provides you with emotional resilience and mental clarity to persevere. It strengthens your resolve and equips you with a reserve to replenish yourself as you build.

If your mind, body, and spirit are out of balance, you become frustrated more quickly and are less able to listen and pivot. If you are tired and beaten down, you are less likely to approach situations and people with optimism and a mindset of abundance. Look at what happened to me. I wasn't pouring into myself, and being perpetually tired and stressed of course affected my ability to show up in other areas of life. When you are fatigued and overwhelmed, you have less capacity to think creatively and to reason. Science tells us we do not think as clearly or remember things as well when we are very stressed. You may misread moments and become defensive and threaten healthy relationships. In fact, research finds that when we are consistently and extremely stressed, we are more likely to perceive something as negative or dangerous, even if it's not. Stress makes us want to isolate, even though being around supportive people can help alleviate distress. All this can jeopardize your village and the work you've put in, not to mention your relationship with yourself!

On the other hand, a person who shows up well—in body, mind, and spirit—is balanced and grounded. They begin to attract the love, the healthy friendships, the quality business partnerships that they've longed for, because light attracts light. People who tend to their needs and refill their own cup have the resources to extend themselves to others in the best of ways. They have a way of speaking to themselves and others with love, kindness, and grace. When a setback comes, they are emotionally and mentally equipped to see the impediment not as failure but as an opportunity to learn lessons, which enables them to be more purposeful and intentional builders. They are present and listening, connected to their own heart and purpose while also open to the experiences and emotions of others. Well villagers are also better able to seek common ground. Challenges are viewed as continuous growth and pivot opportunities, not as failures or the end. Well villagers can more easily see things as they actually are—in proportion. Practicing self-care makes all the hard stuff much easier to tackle, because we are optimistic and clear, a mindset that is linked to lower levels of stress hormones. It's an upward spiral. Everyone wins.

Engaging in self-care also feeds assurance, because when we are well, we trust in our ability to execute on things. We feel prepared to handle whatever the day will bring. We are less likely to feel insecure and competitive when talented people enter the fold, less tempted to question ourselves or rip ourselves apart when mistakes happen. Instead, we interact with a loving assurance, knowing that creating opportunities for others does not take away from our opportunities but instead creates a ripple effect of good energy and opportunity to be shared. The good karma flows back to you and permeates all that you touch.

A person in pursuit of wellness also possesses humility, the ability to resist the impulse to always be the loudest voice in the room or to minimize other people's gifts. A person who has prioritized self-care (as well as the essential soul work discussed in chapter 2) operates in humility and in harmony with others. A humble villager understands that whatever success they've garnered is due to their hard work, vision, and a village of people who supported them. They understand that "self-made" is a myth and that goals and visions have a greater possibility of being actualized with a village-made mindset. Humility also allows you the ability to evolve, to constantly learn and to be open to being taught. Even the most confident leader must open themselves up to meaningful feedback, to not feel threatened when they are in a room with other powerful and impactful people.

All this is wonderful in theory, of course, but in order to achieve the ideal we must confront and push back against some of the realities that make it difficult to get well and work well. First, our country is entrenched in unhealthy constructs that are deemed normal—a never-rest mindset that, until very recently, prized the relentless hustle. A few years ago, a trend took hold that celebrated the grind culture. It even had a hashtag: #TeamNoSleep. Being booked and busy meant you were in pursuit of your dreams. Having zero boundaries became normalized. Even when you tried to achieve a work-life balance, there was a great deal of judgment around rest and the trend of "the soft life." It sent a message to the entrepreneur community: If you weren't grinding, you did not possess determination and grit to "win."

Second, we live in a capitalistic society that prioritizes profit and production. There is nothing wrong with being profitable and productive—businesses should excel at both. But valuing profit above all else crowds out the human part of the equation; worshipping at the altar of production devalues the experience of the people creating the profit and doing the work. If we are not mindful of how villagers are feeling, and if we do not care for the full person, the systems will favor decisions and behaviors that prioritize profit. Burnout and discontent for those engaged in the work will be the default.

On top of that, we must state the obvious: For many Black entrepreneurs, the drive to work excessively with little to no room for self-care stems from economic necessity and survival. Centuries of white supremacy have left our people economically behind. Systemic inequities and structural racism burden us with additional bars to entry that we must clear. Most of the business owners I have worked with are first-generation college graduates and first-generation entrepreneurs, and we are all building our planes as we fly them. We are determined and beyond capable, but given the additional bars to entry, many of us are running on fumes. People of color in the workplace have a higher risk of burnout compared to white people. And women of color and female ethnic minorities are more likely to experience burnout compared to women of the ethnic majority, according to a Deloitte *Women @ Work* 2022 report. One reason for this difference: Women of color experience higher incidences of microaggressions and harassment, and the psychic toll is draining. In addition, women of color, as well as LGBTQ+ people, feel far less comfortable speaking about their mental health in the workplace compared to those who are not members of a marginalized group. People who are historically disenfranchised often already feel underestimated and fear that disclosing a perceived weakness could adversely affect their career. Remember the story about nearly losing the Rockefeller grant? Well, that certainly impacted my stress levels—I didn't want an issue that wasn't my fault and totally out of my hands to make partners think I was incapable and unqualified.

All this underscores why it is so important to take a communal, people-based approach to building a business and for leaders to encourage practices that normalize self-care and a safe, inclusive environment. When everyone is chipping in and being supportive, this allows individuals the ability and time to care for their needs so they can show up healthy for each other. In a community where self-care is prioritized, there is compounded prosperity, support, and goodness for all.

When we don't operate this way, it stunts growth. If we don't prioritize self-care and understand how tightly it is tethered to the health of the community and the business, we will experience the same outcomes, over and over—burnout, poor work culture, high turnover. As a country, I believe that is where we are now. Our economic systems are set up for profit above all else, which practically mandates that corporate leaders value earnings and growth at all costs over employee wellness. For that reason, we are being led by people who are unwell, which in turn creates a workforce that is depleted and disconnected from a greater purpose and from each other. Leaders are showing up as cynical, unhinged, and separated from the interest and well-being of their constituents. If we continue to have people in positions of influence who are not well and not prioritizing collective care for themselves and their communities, our villages will not change. Systems will not change. The body of the country will continue to operate in an unwell state, neglecting our humanity and our peace.

The day after my doctor cautioned me about my physical health, I met with my therapist and told her how I was honestly feeling: I couldn't think clearly, I didn't feel like I was in my body, and I was worried about my lack of sleep. I couldn't get a full night's rest because I consistently woke up at 3:00 a.m. with my mind racing and full of worry about every little thing. I had a hard time sustaining joy. My therapist had been gently urging me to prioritize my wellness for several months. She understood that depression was looming and that I was physically and mentally burned out, and she agreed right away to fill out paperwork for me to take a monthlong leave of absence from GADOE. I felt a rush of relief . . . and anxiety. I'd never taken that much time off work—I very rarely took off any days—but I embraced the time to fill my cup. My therapist's support helped me understand that I was not being soft or extra. While I knew that what I was feeling was real, having her back me was validating. This was not about strength or weakness; this was about survival and restoring what we are all meant to exist in: wellness of spirit and body.

During this time, I did a hard reset. I embraced self-care like it was my job (of course I did). I got back to my daily self-love habits. I juiced in the mornings to get my essential nutrients—something I'd been doing for years but had let lapse. I cooked myself actual meals instead of inhaling quick, heavily processed foods. I went for long walks and bike rides. I journaled and daydreamed. I connected with my close friends and family who brought me joy.

In therapy, I continued to practice giving myself grace, which helped me rein in the runaway train of anxiety and perfectionism. I worked on becoming aware of my thoughts and emotions and mindful about what was triggering a feeling of fear or defeat so I could work through it. Sometimes it's our own thoughts and emotions (as opposed to an outside event) that can open the firehouse of stress hormones. If we do not have tools to move from anxiety and fear to a place of calm and safety—methods like breathing, affirmations, exercise, prayer, music, or whatever soothes us—we slowly lose our energy, our light dims, our confidence shrinks. I am lucky that I had a village in my corner who nourished me with a steady diet of belief in my worthiness, voices of tenderness that would intermingle with my own self-talk. I can always hear my grandmother Josephine's voice—loving and believable, soothing me and reaffirming my worth when I need it most. I can close my eyes and see my mother's smile and feel her comfort come over me. I adopted some wellness modalities introduced to me by Dr. Crystal Jones, an incredible sound and breath alchemist and spiritual adviser. She took me to a sound bath—a meditative experience where you listen to sound vibrations to relax—which helped ground me comfortably and solidly in my body and surrender the negative thoughts.

But the most important tool I learned from Dr. Crystal was mindful breathing. Through slow and controlled breathwork, I discovered how to be in tune with my body, to interpret the muscle signals and energy shifts and other "tells" that I am stressed. It allowed me to shut the door on the waves of anxiety, letting the stress flow through me without taking up residence. And I could do it anywhere, anytime. (I recently learned that deep breathing stimulates the vagus nerve, which in turn activates our body's calming mechanisms, essentially turning off the tap of fight-or-flight stress hormones.)

Day by day, I practiced the wellness strategies that spoke to me. Sure enough, with each day that passed, I became more in tune with myself. I understood without a doubt that self-care was not a sign of weakness but an essential component to being in alignment, of self-preservation. When I was in the throes of my most unhealthy space, I saw intentional days off as an interruption rather than a reset. Now, I see them as a necessity. In the moments of clarity that I hadn't had in months, it hit me that other entrepreneurs had to be experiencing similar waves of anxiety, burnout, or decision fatigue.

When I returned to work, my team and I surveyed the dozens of business owners we worked with and found that 48 percent of them were experiencing burnout—they were physically and mentally at their breaking point as a result of their work life. Thirty-two percent acknowledged depression, and 56 percent reported they were suffering from decision fatigue, a state of mental overload where making choices feels overwhelming. In a world that glorifies hustle, we were all pushing ourselves to exhaustion. I'd certainly pushed myself to the brink, and I couldn't do that anymore if I was going to build a healthy, sustainable village. I had to model the behaviors and create the practices that would let the team know that not only is it merely OK to rest and replenish, but it is also what we deserve. But it's hugely difficult to do so when laboring under poor conditions, struggling on your own with no support or shared resources. The antidote: living and working and recharging within community, where there is abundance of resources and where there's a net to catch you.

In 2020, when I created the Village Retail and Our Village United, I took everything I'd learned from my burnout experience and built the company with a wellness focus, with a people-centered, caring approach as the roots of the enterprises. I hired on-staff therapists for the team to access at no cost. I instituted a "no email on weekend" policy, which I made sure to model by not sending out or answering emails on weekends (unless there was a specific project that required it). I start our team meetings with ten to fifteen minutes of a wellness practice chosen by a team leader—journaling, meditating, listening to a playlist, you name it. My staff know that this is their moment, a gift of time and attention to feel my appreciation and to explore what they need to feel whole and connected to one another; it's an opportunity to generate a mindset of harmony and gratitude before we focus on business. Team members love to create connection and wellness moments by recalling fun and loving memories; playing inspirational videos, like an inspiring short TED talk; and expressing gratitude. We now incorporate wellness into all our programming with Our Village United. In addition to wellness classes, entrepreneurs in the village have access to a licensed therapist for one-on-one sessions and small-group wellness coaching sessions.

At the Village Market, I also launched an event called HER Village, which brought in Black therapists, doctors, nutritionists, fitness professionals, and experts trained in alternative healing modalities—breathwork, energy work, yoga—to introduce the guests to a variety of ways to tend to their bodies and minds. Staff and the owners we work with have indicated in surveys that these wellness components are critical to their ability to manage stress and anxiety and avoid burnout. I believe that a big reason my enterprises have been as successful as they are is because I have woven self-care into the business model.

From a purely business standpoint, prioritizing the mental and emotional wellness of your staff can help your bottom line. Studies show that people whose jobs allow them the time and flexibility to take care of themselves in order to achieve a work-life balance perform better in their jobs and report better job satisfaction. That translates into lower turnover rates and higher productivity for the business—a win-win. Futurists and builders—anyone in a leadership position—should invest in healing modalities and wellness practices, as well as leadership styles that make employees feel valued. Employees who receive validation and appreciation from their managers experience lower rates of burnout, improved emotions, and a stronger connection to their coworkers, according to a 2023 Gallup/Workhuman survey.[*] At my businesses and my nonprofit, I offer paid wellness days, no questions asked. This encourages a climate where it's OK to take a day off, to be vulnerable, to not be at your best 24/7. It brings humanity to the workplace and allows each of us to do the important work of self-care without it sending the signal that we're just not up to the task.

For years in the Black community, there was hesitation about therapy and a fear of discussing mental health. There is pressure to

---

[*] The World Health Organization defines "burnout" as chronic workplace stress characterized by feelings of exhaustion, a mental distancing from one's job (feelings of negativism and cynicism), and reduced professional efficacy.

present a strong facade to the world, to not show weakness or that you're different in any way (this includes queerness) for fear that you might limit your opportunities for growth. As misguided as these beliefs are, it's understandable why they have staying power. As bell hooks reminds us in *All About Love*, the things that Black people have been taught by their parents and community to avoid were often shunned out of love and protection, out of wanting to keep our people safe. But the instinct to hold it all in tends to isolate us and take us away from community.

There is also the idea that if you seek out mental health help, it sends a message that you lack faith that God will answer all your needs or that it's an invitation for someone to *be in your business*. I understand this reluctance. But, I'd say, trust that God made good therapists—just like good doctors. Because of platforms like *Therapy for Black Girls*, founded by my dear friend Dr. Joy Bradford Harden, I believe the perceptions and stigmas of therapy are shifting. She pioneered a space for representation and access for Black women therapists and Black women seeking therapists. Because of this, and because more of us are openly speaking about our positive experiences with therapy, many are starting to believe that you can have a reverence for God *and* seek out therapy—the two are not mutually exclusive but are often a beautiful pairing. (And if there is a time for someone to "be in your business," it's with a therapist.)

I am also acutely aware of the medical bias that exists and persists in our system. Black people are significantly less likely to access mental health services, receive prescription medications for mental health, or be treated for depression compared to white people. Some of these disparities are because Black people are not taken seriously when we visit doctors and discuss our symptoms. Research finds that white health practitioners are less likely to perceive facial expressions of pain in Black patients compared to white patients. And doctors routinely react with more skepticism and judgment toward Black patients than white, studies show.

But treatment gaps also exist because of a long-standing distrust in the goodness and fairness of our medical system. Our country has a history of racialized medical abuse. I was horrified to read about a prominent nineteenth-century physician who attributed enslaved people's efforts for freedom to a mental condition called "drapetomania." The idea that Black Americans harbor made-up psychological illnesses is all the more ludicrous and devastating when you consider that enslavement and discrimination inflict real psychological trauma, not only for the person experiencing the abuse but quite possibly, too, in adaptive behaviors that can get passed from generation to generation. Clinical psychologist Joy DeGruy, PhD, has identified this legacy of violence as posttraumatic slave syndrome, which theorizes that some Black people and communities have internalized harmful mindsets and behaviors (hopelessness, cynicism, low self-worth, learned helplessness) as a response to surviving generations of past and continued oppression and that intentional individual and community healing is needed to shift into more positive outlooks and behaviors.

There is also good evidence that the biological effects of racism and trauma endure, getting passed from generation to generation, resulting in increased chronic illness, chronic pain, and depression. The emerging science of epigenetics—heritable traits in gene structures that can affect how they get expressed (i.e., getting turned on or off) in response to environmental factors (such as stress and nutrition)—suggests that children and grandchildren of war veterans, Holocaust survivors, and enslaved Black Americans, as well as Indigenous Americans with historical trauma, have inherited some effects of the trauma. Today, we see the deadly effects of systemic racism and medical bias: pregnancy-related deaths for Black women are three times higher than for white women. Babies born to Black women are more likely to be low birth weight or preterm or to die from medical complications shortly after birth compared to white babies.

I could go on, but this is all to say it's understandable why Black people distrust a Western-medicine modality such as therapy. Historically, the things that are helpful for white people have been used as tools to harm Black people. This is one reason I offer my staff and entrepreneurs access to Black therapists—to foster the inherent trust that comes from seeing someone who looks like them in the room.

Another barrier to therapy is the lack of access and affordable care. Professional mental health care can be costly, even with insurance, and it's prohibitively so without. Black and Hispanic people persistently have the lowest rates of insurance coverage, barring them from affordable mental health services. Thankfully, there are leaders and organizations working to bridge these gaps. The Loveland Foundation, a nonprofit founded by writer, entrepreneur, and activist Rachel Cargle, provides free therapy to Black women and girls, along with fellowships and residency programs for women of color seeking their counseling licenses. The Boris Lawrence Henson Foundation, cofounded by Taraji P. Henson (named for her late father), offers Black participants no- and low-cost therapy with culturally competent practitioners. It's so critical for people with a microphone to speak up in support of caring for ourselves in this way. I also love the work that Black Men Heal is doing, removing financial and cultural barriers for Black men to better care for their mental health. In addition to offering free counseling, the organization pushes back against the racial and gender norm that Black men must be tough and fearless in the face of struggle. Reframing strength and masculinity as something that includes being vulnerable helps support and celebrate the men in the village, relieving them of the burden of silence, stoicism, and isolation.

It doesn't help that our culture packages self-care as something only available to those with significant discretionary income. Self-care has been commodified and fed to us as achievable through pricey wellness retreats and expensive spa treatments, even though caring for yourself does not require a first-class flight to a five-star resort with an infinity pool in an exotic place (although those things are certainly nice if you decide to indulge!). At its core, self-care is the way that you speak to yourself; it is the things you do for yourself that are medicine for your soul. If you can (assuming your movements aren't restricted), stretch or walk outside or lie on a blanket on the grass in a park, laughing with someone you love. Talk to God, blast music, dance. Self-care does not come with a price tag that we have to recover from. If you cannot afford or don't have time for a meditation retreat, there are loads of videos on YouTube on how to meditate or quiet your mind and harness the power of manifestation. Simply saying no to uninspiring social plans, enforcing a no-work zone, and learning how to not be triggered by FOMO for one day each weekend so you can do whatever the heck you want is self-care. Ultimately, it is whatever you need that allows you to show up as your fullest self.

I will say that despite the commodification of self-care, the wellness movement in our community has been refreshing and encouraging. So many of us have accepted that one of our generation's roles is to disrupt the dogma of historically Eurocentric models of sacrificing Black bodies and souls for the pursuit of success. We are on a path of generational healing. Rest Is Revolution and the soft life movement have gained steam in the Black community over the last several years and have helped root this idea in our collective consciousness, positioning rest, self-love, and gentleness as acts of preservation and justice for the Black community, all without having to give up success or upward mobility. Tricia Hersey's Nap Ministry is a loud voice in this arena, advocating for rest as a form of resistance, a disruptor of the grind culture and liberation for generations of Black Americans who have been forced into labor and enslavement.

It is often challenging to figure out how to embed and prioritize wellness while we are in the pursuit of building. I understand feeling so overwhelmed that the thought of adding self-care to your to-do list feels like one more thing you don't have time for. But whatever time and energy you invest in yourself will pay you back tenfold. You do not have to take a forced leave of absence like I did (though if you need to and you have the opportunity, consider gifting yourself some time off). Curate your day in such a way that it begins with centering you, your mind, your heart, and create internal check-in breaks or breathwork throughout the day. Breathwork takes ten seconds, which you can easily do at stoplights on your way to and from a meeting; a meditation or prayer takes one to five minutes, the time it takes to steep your morning tea or sip your coffee. Be protective of how you end your nights; allow a clear disconnection between you and the business. Whether you turn off your phone or crawl into bed with a book, it's important to connect with *yourself* at the end of the day. There has to be time for your mind to breathe.

For people who have spent their life sacrificing and pursuing their dreams, the shift from go-go-go to intentional rest and recover is not always easy. I have had entrepreneurs share that they want to be village minded and embody a wellness mindset, but they are in survival mode and have no idea how they can press pause for themselves, let alone help anyone else. To them I say, lean on your village. Your community can and should be an essential partner in Operation Self-Care. People in need can be of tremendous assistance to one another. Whether it's pooling resources, setting intentional gratitude calls, collaborating to bring in a wellness coach, or planning a walk or hike meetup, being in a community of like-minded people is essential to shifting your mindset.

Anything worthwhile is not easy. Good work will challenge you. You will be stretched to an uncomfortable place. When it comes to entrepreneurship, you can have the best day of your life and the worst day of your life in a single email thread. That's a lot of emotion to grapple with over and over again, and if you don't have tools to keep your mind from spinning, you become reactive instead of proactive, responding with impatience rather than grace and reason. I encourage my friends, team members, and businesses in the village to incorporate self-care as preventive care, *before* the crisis hits. We are told not to wait until we're sick to go to the doctor, to get regular checkups. Self-care is no different. Resist waiting until things are perfect in your life or until you reach a certain milestone or level of success to begin. Your success is tethered to how well you love and commit to loving and nurturing yourself. And it is essential for doing the work that will set up the community for prosperity, today and decades in the future. This revolutionary act will require our dedication and steadfastness.

## HOW I FILL MY CUP

While everyone's self-care plan looks different, I'm sharing a few of my wellness practices with you so you can get some ideas if you'd like. I think of self-care in the same way my grandmothers, Josephine and Bobbie, approach cooking—you have to make the dish your own. Someone can give you a recipe, but it won't taste as good if you don't throw in what you love. Like a good gumbo, figure out what works for you. I don't need you to do any of the things I'm listing below. I need you—*you* need you—to be in harmony and do what feels right for you. Maybe you can take some inspiration from my practice; maybe it'll just illuminate what could be helpful with yours!

**I pray. First thing, last thing, and throughout the day.** Prayer is my morning OJ. I seek God for all things, major and minor, and I thank God throughout the day, a practice that I have had since I was a child. God is my most sacred relationship, and my time in prayer is when I feel the safest and most loved. It gives me the confidence and clarity to keep taking the steps I am meant to take in my purpose. I see God in my relationships with people and in places as I go about my day and during my many travels—a connected conversation with a kindred spirit, walking down a vibrant city street and musing through a park.

**I protect my mornings.** It is my most sacred time of the day
that I hoard for myself. I wake up early, naturally around 4:30
or 5:00 a.m., and check in with myself to see how my body
feels and to determine what I feel like I need that day. It's my
time with God and myself. I speak kind and loving words to
myself, and I get ahead of any anxieties by running through
any upcoming projects or meetings that make me anxious.
If it's a meeting, I envision how I want that interaction to
go, how I want to feel, and how I want the other person to
feel, and then I picture myself walking away with clarity and
direction. Next, I drink my water. I read. I head to the gym
and I finish up with a walk.

**I am intentional about what I feed my body.** The majority of
the foods I eat are unprocessed, sugar-free (or contain very
little added sugar), and living foods, meaning they are as close
to their natural form as possible (organic, mostly plant based,
bursting in nutrients). Seeing my mother suffer with lupus put
me on a health journey that impacts me to this day. I fill up on
foods that are unaltered and low in acid (vegetables and herbs)
as well as anti-inflammatory foods (berries, nuts and seeds,
leafy veggies, whole grains), which can help prevent and even
treat diseases, including autoimmune conditions. Many people
are told that a condition just "runs in the family" and they
are prescribed a drug to treat it, when they could control or
reverse it by eating less or more of certain foods. Decades of
research prove that a diet rich in plants and low in unhealthy
fats (dairy, red meat) and sugar is linked to a lower risk of
heart disease, diabetes, and dementia. I eat this way not only
for my physical health but also for my mood. A high-carb,
high-sugar diet increases the risk of depression and anxiety
(probably because sugars spike blood sugar and certain
hormones, which sets off a balance-disrupting roller coaster

of highs and lows). You do not have to eat like a rabbit (as my grandma says), adhering to a 100 percent plant-based diet, to reap the benefits. Just start with one small change at a time.

**I move my body, somehow.** Exercise saves me, boosting my mood and reconnecting me to my body in a positive relationship. Sometimes I'll hike on a trail alongside the Chattahoochee River. Sometimes I'll bike through downtown Atlanta or Piedmont Park. Other times I'll hit a Peloton class to destress and recenter my thoughts (shout-out to the incredible Tunde Oyeneyin, an instructor whose energy and positivity push me to increase my resistance and to ride harder) or schedule a morning workout session with my trainer, Frederick. You've surely read about all the ways exercise is good for our bodies and minds. It's especially helpful at purging cortisol, the stress hormone. Any movement counts. Even a quickie stretch session or leisurely walk around the block is a beautiful act of self-care and love.

**I let therapy mend my heart.** My first experience with therapy was when my mother transitioned after a nearly ten-year battle against lupus and, later, a diagnosis of breast cancer. I hadn't tried therapy before then, but I was desperate for any alleviation of my pain and grief. So I searched grief therapists within my health provider's network and found a holistic therapy center. My first therapist was a white woman in her late twenties. Her name was Jessica and we were around the same age. Her brown eyes were soft and warm, and her overall presence was comforting. I was so depleted by grief that I honestly don't remember much of our sessions. I was filled with uncertainty for my life, anger with God, and so much sadness. Sadness for my then nine-year-old sister; sadness for my brother; sadness for my nephew, who was three at the time; and sadness for my grandmother, who had lost her first child. Sadness for myself. I was drowning in sadness. I didn't know how *to do* therapy, but I consistently showed up for my sessions, heartbroken and broken—when I could talk, I talked, and when I could only cry, I cried. It became my sacred space, and I credit Jessica for helping me during a very difficult time in my life. She remained my therapist until she moved away. I knew that I wanted to continue seeing a therapist, but this time I did not want to focus specifically on grief; I wanted to explore a number of things that loomed in my mind and were taking up residence in my spirit. Through a recommendation from a friend, I was connected to a brilliant Black woman therapist with whom I felt safe. It was both similar and different from my time with Jessica, but what stood out the most was her ability to understand without my having to overly explain cultural differences. There was a connection and comfort in the similar experiences of being Black and being women. My current therapist, Thandie, often reminds me when I need to hear it most: "This time is your time. You do not have to censor what you say. You can be free to feel." Her laugh, the warmth in her eyes, and her loving nudge to go deeper have cradled me as I journey. Self-care is leaning into time that is just for you, time that allows you to breathe easy and feel the feels and receive the reassurance that you will not only survive but that you'll also find harmony again.

**I set hard-and-fast rules around work.** This simple practice shifted my entire life. Before I had work boundaries, everything was bleeding into everything else. It wasn't unusual to wake up to a text at 5:00 a.m. or to work all weekend. It was the culture I'd inadvertently set for my team, too, and while we accomplished great work during that time, we did not have needed boundaries. Now, I have hard start and stop times for work, and when I stick to them (which is almost always, unless we're working on a time-sensitive project), it sends a message to my team that they, too, should have work-life separation. I'm thrilled to write that it is a rarity for anyone to work on the weekend or answer an email at night. What has helped me most in setting work boundaries is being very direct with people; my nos are my nos. It helps avoid stressful miscommunications, which can eat up precious time and energy. If I cannot meet, I do not meet. If it has to wait until tomorrow, my practice is to trust that tomorrow is the perfect time.

I cannot emphasize enough that self-care is not just for the self (despite its name), nor is it an end point. We are not meant to find ease and joy only to sit back and bask in them, end of story. It's not just a box to check. We are becoming—and *staying*—well so we can be restored and invigorated for our purpose, for our village-made purpose, in unity with other villagers who share the mission. We take care of ourselves so we can exist in a place of clarity and awareness and alignment. It gives us the ability to trust that when things feel off, they are off. It lets us know when we need a day and to take a day without regrets. Self-care empowers us to have awareness when we mishandled situations and to see that expressing forgiveness is a powerful act of leadership. It helps us be better communicators with our teams, our community, and the people we love. When a community centers wellness, it helps us truly love and show up for one another. It positions us to collaborate, to function as a village.

We all possess an inner light. Self-care allows our light to shine more brightly, and when we find our light growing dim, we have the tools, the community, and the sacred time to nourish the light within us. And when the community is in need of light during dark times, those who are well will shine like the North Star and give the community hope that this, too, shall pass. We understand that as we build and expand, true success is achieved when we enhance health. If we prioritize health, wealth and good things will follow.

## Reflection Questions

* Do you regularly schedule time for yourself to rest, meditate, sweat, or socialize? If not, why not? If so, how does it make you feel to prioritize yourself?

* How do busy or tough times affect your self-care routines?

* What are some things you wish you could find more time for? What is holding you back from prioritizing those activities?

* How does your work suffer when you don't make time for yourself?

* How do your relationships (friendships, coworkers, family) suffer when you don't center your own needs?

* What healthy practice can you set up within your business to ensure a healthy environment for your staff and yourself?

* What is your vision for a healthy, loving community? What does it feel like? How do you feel?

* How can you create healthy pathways in your community?

# SEVEN

# Generational Wealth and Pathways to Parity

THIS CHAPTER IS ABOUT BUILDING GENERATIONAL WEALTH FOR yourself, your loved ones, and your beloved community. But it is not simply about getting rich. It is about creating a better existence and closing the racial wealth gap in a way that challenges the status quo and centers on a more fundamental goal: freedom and parity for all Black people. It's about being the person in your family and professional community who can take a collective approach and improve the circumstances of those who are alive now and for those who will be here after you are gone. There's this adage I love: "The true meaning of life is to plant trees under those whose shade you do not expect to sit." The shade for future generations moves the starting line up. It provides them with reserves and arms them with access and ownership. What the ancestors built and overcame, we reap. We are nourished from the harvest of their unimaginable sacrifices. It is on us to do the same for the next generation. It is a responsibility and an honor.

I did not come from wealth. There was no college fund or starter savings account or family vacations. My mother worked at a factory in Sardis, Mississippi, called Hygiene Industries—the largest curtain company in the industry—making a little over $5 an hour on the production line. My dad worked a seasonal job at Thermos, making $5.10 an hour assembling thermoses each day (the company is currently valued at $5.14 billion). Combined, my parents made roughly $10 an hour. They had two hard financial objectives: to buy a house and to ensure their three children never lacked anything they needed.

My father worked fourteen-hour days, six days a week, signing up for all the overtime he could. During the months he wasn't employed at Thermos, he repaired cars for supplemental income. My mother often worked overtime for additional income. Together, they brought home about $44,000 a year. We lived in a single-bedroom rental without indoor plumbing and insulation. My siblings and I bundled up during icy winters and learned to keep our feet on the bed to avoid the rat snakes slithering across the floor. In their late twenties, my parents landed jobs at local factories that paid them more sustainable wages, and they were able to start saving money for the first time. When I was nine, they purchased their first home for $33,000. My maternal grandmother, who had excellent credit, served as the cosigner. It was a three-bedroom home sitting on a quarter acre of land, with large pecan trees, beautiful hardwood floors, and spacious rooms with a lot of windows. It embodied the dreams my parents had for their first home.

My parents had defied the odds and begun their climb of upward mobility. It was an especially remarkable achievement given the structural racism of the housing market in America, and in the Deep South in particular. They faced the legacy of redlining—a discriminatory practice that began in the 1930s that labeled Black buyers and Black neighborhoods as too "risky" for a home mortgage loan—and predatory loan practices, in which buyers who *could* afford standard loans were coerced into subprime loans at higher interest rates. My parents were repeatedly denied a mortgage loan, and it ultimately took village support to make it all happen. My great-grandmother called her friend Ms. Peaches, who worked for the white sellers as their maid. Ms. Peaches vouched for my parents, and the sellers made a call to the lender. Only then were my parents able to start the process of buying the house.

Financially, they knew they could manage the mortgage because they had been taught fundamental, safe financial practices by their own parents. My grandma Bobbie taught my father to never take more than he could pay back, to always pay on time, and to maintain good credit. My grandmother Josephine raised my mother to always live a little below her means so she could have a financial cushion and avoid borrowing. My parents used those lessons to provide a financial foundation for us, and thanks to their hard work and dedication, over time we became a $100,000 combined-income household with three children who were eyeing college.

Seeing what they overcame was inspiring and heartbreaking all at once. They triumphed against discriminatory practices, yes, but they had to overcome so much relative to white folks in the area. Homeownership is often the first step in creating generational wealth. It's a hallmark of the American dream: having a safe place to raise a family. It's also a way to make things more obtainable for the next generation so they can pursue their dreams. Although my parents could not afford to gift me a down payment for a home or business, they gave me clear financial values and a foundation from which to build. I knew that homeownership was attainable for me because my parents showed me the way. I saw my grandmother Bobbie run her own business, so I knew that being a business owner was also something I could achieve.

But in their quest for homeownership, my father taught me that wealth and freedom cannot be conflated. He told me he was proud of owning a home because he'd worked hard for it, but that wasn't the same as freedom. Freedom, he explained, is not something material; true freedom happens when barriers are eradicated that systemically keep Black people in a "place." Fulfilling a financial dream alone does not lead to the ultimate goal of being free as Black people, of achieving parity and shared prosperity. Freedom is also being able to validate yourself without proximity or adjacency to whiteness.

I began my climb toward upward mobility, but I never forgot my dad's distinction between wealth and freedom or my parents' financial modeling. I worked extremely hard and lived beneath my means ("so your back won't be against the wall," my father advised). I saved money and bought a home as soon as I could afford to, relying on my village for support. My dear friend Tasha lent me the extra cash that I needed, and I leaned on my mentor, Jeanette Francis-Ferris, and my mortgage officer, Kerry, to walk me through the buying process. When I launched my business, I used money I'd saved so I wouldn't have to borrow; I was terrified of taking on debt, as I'd witnessed the pitfalls of cash advance loans that impacted family members. The whole time, I was fueled by the many conversations with my father about the difference between freedom and financial success. I knew my job was to stay focused on freedom.

As I navigated becoming an entrepreneur, the concept of true freedom for Black people—and how the concept intersected with business—started to take on more meaning. I began to realize just how much the capitalist system wasn't working for Black people. I found myself less willing to lean on the tenets of capitalism, which prioritizes profit over everything else, centers the individual and excludes the collective, and favors competition over collaboration. Wealth is only amassed by a very few and circulated within exclusive circles. I mean, the fact that the wealthiest 1 percent of Americans own about one-third of the nation's wealth tells you everything about whom the system serves. Capitalism works really, really well for those who already have wealth—people and corporations who own a lot of land, real estate, and investments—and it is designed to oppress those who do not yet have ownership or the capital to invest. Capitalism is a major reason why the generational wealth gap between Black and white households began in the first place—and why it's getting worse. Since 1992, the racial wealth gap has widened. Today, for every $100 held by white households, Black households have $15. Since the days of enslavement, capitalism has been racialized in our country. Plantations were, in essence, factories that used enslaved workers to produce goods and services and profits for the plantation owner, who was competing against other plantation owners. Because racism and capitalism grew up together in our country, the practices and policies that developed along the way served those who historically held the most power: white men. In a 1965 speech, Martin Luther King Jr. told us as much, linking racial segregation to cheap labor and profits: "The segregation of the races was really a political stratagem employed by the emerging Bourbon interests in the South to keep the southern masses divided and southern labor the cheapest in the land." The economic legacy of slavery and Jim Crow—systemic racism in the job, financial, and housing sectors; underinvestment in Black businesses; a lack of reparations—is a big reason why the generational wealth gap has remained unchanged for nearly a century and is now widening.

The more I learned about how catastrophic capitalism has been for Black Americans, the more convinced I became that running my businesses with this approach would not lead to the kind of freedom and economic liberty my father spoke of. In capitalism, owners are encouraged to protect the bottom line at all costs—paying employees the bare minimum to drive profits and ignoring the responsibility to improve the livelihoods of workers or to invest in the community as the company becomes successful. Instead, I vowed to find ways to weave village-made values into the financial practices and structures of my enterprises. Like my ancestors had done, I borrowed ideas from group economics: collectively pooling resources to overcome what one individual cannot accomplish alone. I also began to view community as a resource in and of itself. The village is capital in the sense that it is *social* capital. Community is the secret sauce that can overcome the inequities of capitalism. In the same way that it takes money to make more money, it takes community to benefit the whole community. This is the essence of group economics, that the sum of everyone together is larger and more powerful than any single person on their own. I embraced *social entrepreneurship*, a way of operating a for-profit business that leverages profits for a direct and positive impact on the community. I created a nonprofit that would hold hands with the retail store and launch budding entrepreneurs into an equitable ecosystem. I wanted the entrepreneurs in the village to be wildly successful and profitable, of course, to help reverse the racial wealth gap, *but only by using practices that are inclusive, sustainable, and truly freedom bound.* That was my biggest realization: *Unless wealth is generated intentionally and allows its influence and access to undergird a movement for all Black people, it will not move the collective needle.* It just can't.

We need major policy changes as well that are aimed at reducing discriminatory practices or promoting economic equity, but we cannot afford to wait for these solutions. If things continue the way they are, it will take well over three hundred years by some estimates for Black families to amass the same amount of wealth as white households. We must move away from the self-made and individualistic model and shift to a communal one, an approach geared at helping Black Americans succeed and lifting up other Black Americans. The beauty of structuring businesses collectively and equitably is that it is actually less financially risky and more prosperous for the community than if we build using the capitalist system. Collective models (which I explain on page 168) help ensure that you are not shouldering all the operating costs alone. Basically, these models fairly distribute profit among the members and focus on local economic development, aka reinvesting money back into the community. Now, building this way may lessen the profit in the short term: Because you are committing to dispensing profit equitably, it may take longer to hit certain financial goals. But when it comes to the wealth and health of the company team and the community, I believe it is *the* most sustainable strategy. After all, you're literally strengthening your village as you build.

For those who struggle with the notion that someone who "does good" shouldn't care about financial success, or for those who feel guilt or shame about making money and living well, I offer this: For communities to thrive, the work *needs* to be profitable. Power, influence, and money are entwined in our society. A person who fights for the liberation of a community should be liberated themselves. It may feel uncomfortable at first, but you can absolutely do good and make money at the same time. You can feel pride in what you have accumulated and in the example you set. Your success—and how you utilize it for the village—shows others what is possible for them as well as for the community.

Another way to think about it: If you are in a strong financial position, you can do more for the village. We've seen Black leaders harness their economic and social positions to better the community and fuel movements. It took fundraising and donations from people such as Harry Belafonte, Sidney Poitier, and Mollie Moon (a Black socialite and civil rights activist) to progress the civil rights movement. The many marches and bus boycotts led by Dr. King, Ella Baker (a cofounder of the Southern Christian Leadership Conference [SCLC] and the Student Nonviolent Coordinating Committee [SNCC]), Diane Nash (an activist and cofounder of SNCC), Bayard Rustin (a key organizer for the 1963 March on Washington for Jobs and Freedom), and countless other faithful leaders weren't free. Someone had to pay for the food, transportation, gas, and lodging. Money delivers agency, opportunity, and power—and with it a great responsibility, I believe, to accumulate it and use it wisely and equitably.

# THE HARD FACTS: THE WEALTH GAP

I do not like to dwell too long on the barriers facing Black entrepreneurs—it can be paralyzing to read about the disparities, to feel like you are gasping for air. But I also believe that we must know the things we are fighting against if we are to work toward the solutions. Much like the barriers my parents faced in their journey to homeownership, entrepreneurs face a similar set of systemic obstacles. It's not due to lack of talent or personal failure that so many Black entrepreneurs struggle to build and scale; it's about the cards stacked *against* them. It's easy to attribute any kind of "failing" to yourself, to let shame lead your perspective, but I promise the roots of the inequities are responsible.

When we look at the big picture of wealth and generational wealth, the inequities are glaring. In 2019, the median wealth of Black households in the United States was $24,100, compared to $189,100 for white households. Remember that wealth is more than annual income—it includes the value of a person's or a business's assets (minus debts), including investments, real estate, businesses, trusts, and savings. The wealth that gets passed down from generation to generation is called generational wealth. Wealth and generational wealth matter greatly for the obvious reasons. In terms of homeownership and personal investment, heirs have more disposable income because they aren't spending a large portion of their paychecks on rent or mortgages. This means they can invest money in retirement accounts to secure their futures; they can afford to take time off and spend more on caring for their body and spirit; and they can more easily ride out the tough times—like recessions and periods of inflation—and bounce back. After the 2008 recession, when all households declined in wealth, white households began to rebound in 2010, whereas Black households have continued to lose wealth.

Clearly, generational wealth is also significant when it comes to building a successful business. Having a financial cushion not only lowers the risks of starting a business, but it also allows you to take *more* risks, which can lead to rapid growth and expansion, and when times are tight, you are better able to hang on and pivot. Black businesses are more likely than white businesses to close after four years, for a wealth (pun intended) of reasons, including barriers to establishing lines of credit and securing small-business loans. (And, incidentally, the costs associated with closing businesses increase the wealth gap!) When you have wealth, you have greater access to low-interest loans because you own investments and real estate as collateral. The more assets you own, the lower the risk to the lender and the more likely they'll take a chance on you. It also gives you far more opportunities to invest in other projects. I know how helpful having assets as collateral is from trying to build my business and from helping other Black entrepreneurs build theirs. The barriers to entry are higher and the stakes are steeper—there is little to no wiggle room for error when you are either just scraping by or are flying solo. Or both. And when you're barely getting by, it is *really* difficult to scale. That's perhaps the biggest benefit of generational wealth: You can jump from being a solopreneur to an employer who can hire.

This radically uneven playing field is why I dreamed of opening an equitable retail space for Black entrepreneurs—I wanted to remove burdens of entry so that founders could focus on their zone of genius, generate more profit, and scale up over time. As I described in chapter 5, the pandemic provided me with the mental clarity and opportunity to turn my vision into reality. It all started with a serendipitous phone call. In mid-2020, I was doing what most businesses were doing: thinking through my pivot strategy to stay afloat amid the uncertainty of an economic downturn. One summer afternoon, I got a call from my friend Kristen telling me about two vacant storefronts at Ponce City Market. Located in the heart of the city along the Atlanta Beltline, near the historic Fourth Ward neighborhood, Ponce City Market is *the* place in Atlanta to showcase and sell your wares and food. Kristen was considering creative opportunities for

food and retail, and she wanted to know if I had interest in partnering with her company, Jamestown. Years before, I'd wanted to
do pop-up markets at Ponce City Market, but there was little buy-in
from the property manager at the time. Since then, Ponce City Market had become a distant thought, though I'd occasionally go with
friends to grab a quick bite or shop for local brands. But on this day,
as Kristen described the vacancies, I started to feel excited.

I thought about the number of Black businesses I could house
there, displaying their unique offerings in an affordable, communal
way. This would be the next-level expansion of the seasonal markets
I'd been hosting, a round-the-clock destination for Black brands and
our diverse clientele. But . . . I also felt some anxiety. Times were
already so difficult, and retail is a tough industry. Adding to that, the
store would be on the second floor of Ponce City Market, when the
majority of the foot traffic was on the first floor.

And yet.

Couldn't it work? At all of the Village Market events, I was blown
away with the quality, the attention to detail, and the uniqueness of
many of the brands. Companies like Savoir Faire, Love Ground Can-
dle, A Few Wood Men, and Weathered Not Worn had been with me
since the early Village Market days, and newer companies like GOAT
by James King, the Muted Home, and World of Unoia (rebranded
PAWS, Peace and Wellness for Dogs) were coming on board—I absolutely loved their offerings. I also knew that, like many entrepreneurs,
they simply needed the opportunity to shine. Having a physical venue
would allow them to get there; their excellent products would do the
rest and allow them to scale.

Most of those entrepreneurs weren't otherwise going to get that
opportunity. Like the majority of Black start-ups, they were laboring
hard to survive, primarily because they had no financial safety net
to cradle them in hard times, no easy access to low-interest loans, no
investments or generational wealth to tap while they waited for the
economic upturn. Yes, the pandemic was proving tough for nearly

all businesses—all small companies suffered a drop in earnings—but by the end of 2020, Black business owners would see losses of earnings 13 percent steeper than their white counterparts. Housing my retail venture at Ponce City Market would be an opportunity to reverse this trend by creating the structural and economic changes that would help close the generational wealth gap. Even with the challenges, it seemed like this could be one way to turn things around.

However, I knew I would have to find a way to build the retail store differently from traditional business models. The big problem for most entrepreneurs was the barriers to entry: large overhead costs such as staffing, market rent, marketing, and e-commerce fees. And importantly, I did not want to take equity in their businesses in exchange for lowering these bars to entry. That's a common strategy, but ownership is power and gives you agency. Historically, Black people's ownership—of property, of land, of businesses, of their own bodies and personhood—has been severely limited and outright stolen. The legacy of this theft is ongoing and underscores the need to increase and preserve Black ownership. The last thing I wanted to do was add to that theft.

## BLACK LAND LOSS: THE NEED TO GAIN GROUND

Something I couldn't escape while considering this physical venture was the idea of property. Land, specifically. The acceleration in the wealth gap between white and Black people over the last century is tied directly to a loss of land ownership, specifically farmland. In 1920, 14 percent of all farms were operated by Black farmers, who owned more than sixteen million acres of crops such as tobacco, cotton, sorghum, and hay, along with grazing livestock. By 2017, that figure had plummeted to 1.7 percent, just half a percent of the country's 895 million acres of farmland. To put it another way, *Black farmers owned more farmland in the Jim Crow South than they do today.* Due to decades of discrimination—the routine denial of US Department of Agriculture (USDA) loans to farmers of color, severely restricting the crops they could grow—over the last century, twelve million acres of Black-owned farmland in the United States have been lost to the tune of an estimated $326 billion.

I learned these stunning facts after joining the Highland Project, founded by my friend Gabrielle Wyatt. Gabrielle is truly a futurist and a builder. She developed the Highland Project—a nonprofit that awards a cohort of Black women innovators $100,000 each—to create multigenerational wealth for Black communities, targeting seven generations ahead. At one of the gatherings, we focused a great deal of thought on the massive land loss and the injustices done to Black farmers to better understand why Black economic mobility continues to be at a standstill. After our session, I immersed myself in the literature and discovered the work of Nathan Rosenberg, who studies agriculture and inequality. In speaking about drivers of racial inequity, Rosenberg puts it this way: "If you want to understand wealth and inequality in this country, you have to understand Black land loss." I did just that, diving deep into the research to piece together the story.

I could not unsee what I read.

In addition to discovering the avalanche of political and economic discrimination against Black farmers, I learned how recent attempts to right the wrongs have been stonewalled. In 2021, the USDA finally acknowledged that the government had illegally refused loans to Black farmers, and Congress approved $3.1 billion in loan forgiveness for a generation of Black farmers. But in 2022, white farmers (led by rancher Sid Miller, who also just happens to be Texas's agriculture commissioner) sued to stop the program, claiming that *white* farmers were being discriminated against based on race. Democrats were forced to rewrite the legislation without reference to race in order to move it incrementally forward (relying on language such as "distressed" and "discriminated" borrowers to distribute $2.2 million). But many Black farmers remain excluded. Senators Cory Booker, Raphael Warnock, Elizabeth Warren, and several others introduced the Justice for Black Farmers Act in January 2023 to help restore land through grants and fund agriculture training and cooperatives (businesses owned by the employees). But between lawsuits to block financial relief and mountains of red tape stalling relief, discrimination persists: In 2022, just over one-third of farmers who identified as Black and applied for loans were approved, compared to 72 percent of farmers who identify as white. Currently, 96 percent of farmers are white, own 98 percent of the acres, and generate 97 percent of farm earnings. What that means is that the vegetable, fruit, meat, and dairy sections of your local grocery store—the ribs and smoked corn being cooked at the family cookout—are mostly grown and owned by white farmers, who benefit from season after season of lucrative local and governmental contracts.

This is just one example out of thousands showing how Black people have been—and continue to be—cut off from ownership in this country. They have little to pass on to their children and their children's children, not because they don't work hard or don't know how to save or invest but because they've been oppressed from growing their wealth. As an owner, you become a producer instead of a consumer, and the wealth that is created in this country stems largely from those who have the ability to own what they produce. What's needed is an increase in *ownership* across all sectors and in all communities—the ability to control your income and retain your money.

In late summer of 2020, I signed the lease for the Village Retail at Ponce City Market. My aim was to use many of the principles of group economics and to operate as a social enterprise, a business model that addresses social or environmental issues—such as food insecurity, climate, poverty, education—while also generating revenue. In essence, a social enterprise operates for two purposes: financial sustainability and social impact. This hybrid approach would keep my business fully aligned with my purpose—to make it easier for people to buy from Black businesses and for Black businesses to increase their profits and, importantly, create something unique, equitable, village oriented, and sustainable in the process. The nuts and bolts: We use a model where the company and the businesses in the store share in sales. When the brands have a good month, we both benefit; when there's a slow month, we both feel it. Placement in the store is very affordable for the small-business owners, as they do not have overhead costs beyond their inventory. If someone has a couple of down months, they aren't removed; they meet with Yolanda, our retail operations manager, and Deana, our retail and e-commerce specialist. We offer coaching and provide the knowledge and assistance needed to formulate an improvement plan. My company's dedicated full-time staff manage the full operations, including build-out, monthly rent, shipping, marketing, photoshoots, and all the day-to-day operations, both onsite and online. So the small businesses are financially responsible for only two things: their shelf fee and the cost of their goods. This enables them to focus on scaling up, to retain more profits for reinvestment, to fine-tune, and to dream up new product lines and community ventures.

And this model *works*. One of our brands was doing about $45,000 sales before she entered the store—today she is doing more than $500,000. As of this writing, the Village Market and the Village Retail has generated $8.8 million in direct sales to Black businesses and has provided a gateway for entrepreneurs to sell their products, generate consistent revenue, and—for those who have made it a focus—quit their full-time jobs to focus on their businesses.

The Village Retail has always been more than retail for me. While it is a protected communal space for Black entrepreneurs to have their brands on the shelves for thousands of customers on a weekly basis, it is also a launch pad for a new generation of Black business owners. It is an incubator for solopreneurs to own and grow their business concepts in ways they couldn't do easily in a traditional capitalist landscape rigged against them. The Village Retail is also an open ecosystem that makes it easy to engage with the local community and to invite in new concepts and dynamic futurists. We've welcomed political figures like Mayor Andre Dickens, authors such as Tabitha Brown, and megastars like Jamie Foxx, who dropped by to shop. We've partnered with corporate businesses, some local and some global, to share resources and create relationships with the villagers. Large companies like Bank of America and Warner Media have purchased products in great volume. Through our partnership with Mastercard, we featured a showroom at *The Jennifer Hudson Show* in Los Angeles, where Jennifer's customers had an opportunity to experience the businesses' products and shop online from us. We've collaborated with big-box retailers such as Target to offer retail readiness classes for the brands in the store, which provide unmatched access for the businesses to expand their dreams. We partner and curate pop-ups with esteemed community partners such as United Way Atlanta, Black Love, and the *Atlanta Journal-Constitution*. These collaborations allow us to feature Village Retail brands at these events, providing them valuable exposure at no cost.

But it wasn't easy.

I will tell you that the first year I opened the Village Retail, we just broke even. Before we opened, I crunched the numbers with my accountant and my fractional CFO to ensure I had a generous grace period, a financial cushion to operate revenue-free during which I could test and refine the model. But because I was shouldering such high start-up costs, the cushion was . . . well, not quite enough. Since I could not afford a second year of not making a profit, I brainstormed with my team ways we could diversify—pop-ups, more events, establishing anchor businesses and working others into rotation—to get us in a healthier financial state. We worked hard to get the model right—keeping it fair and equitable while staying out of the red—so that we could keep the doors open. It was a true start-up journey.

It was really stressful at times, and we all made financial sacrifices and modifications along the way. We had to have tough conversations with the entrepreneurs as we approved the refined model, discussions about how to make the Village Retail a win-win to ensure that our doors stayed open. Some businesses stayed and some did not, but this is true to the start-up journey. When you are striving to build differently, it is important to expect transitions, pivots, losses and gains.

Today, it is a resounding success—and not just because of the financial calculus. We've had thousands of shoppers who represent different cities and countries. The store has consistently generated seven figures in sales, and we are sharing the bounty with the brands of the Village. Even though the beginning was incredibly stressful, we were prepared for growing equitably—and we were ready to pivot as we needed to. Most importantly, to me, we're serving our community and giving both entrepreneurs and consumers access to *amazing* products. Frankly, I love the crazy and creative aspects of this work (most business owners do) and know the best plan usually doesn't materialize with the first go-round. Without the failures and the willingness to pivot in response, you won't arrive at the solutions.

## VILLAGE-LED WAYS TO ECONOMIC PARITY

There are several proven methods to challenge the model of capitalism and bridge inequities in ways that generate inclusivity. My blueprint—a buffet of sorts, borrowing best practices from models that align with my purpose and goals—is one pathway. There are many successful examples from the past and present that can serve as inspiration for futurists and builders motivated by a far reaching, collective approach. After all, the racial wealth gap is not being driven by Black poverty; it is being driven by *a lack of affluence* caused by economic racism. Economic racism perpetuates and reinforces existing racial inequalities, contributing to the socioeconomic marginalization of Black people. Wealth begets wealth. I believe that we can tackle this gap by building scalable, sustainable businesses that center the village.

Here are some of the communal models I have learned from and which inspire the work. As you build, consider how to adapt some of the principles in your models:

* **Group economics.** "Group economics" is an umbrella term that refers to economic practices and ideas that begin and end with the community. In group economics—also called collective economics—the community of people or businesses who share the same economic goal pool their resources to keep money circulating in the community and are intentional about using collective economic power to elevate the community. It is an effective way to create the leverage necessary to overcome the systemic barriers for shared success. At its heart, group economics is about people coming together to accomplish what one person cannot do alone. As I shared in chapter 1, Black Americans have achieved towering economic goals throughout history by combining resources—Greenwood's Black Wall Street, Mound Bayou, Mississippi—and keeping dollars circulating locally within the community. Countries in Africa have been practicing various versions of collective economics for centuries. We've begun to practice group economics in creative ways in the twenty-first century. Getting the community together for Village Market events to buy, amplify, and support Black businesses is an example of group economics. Social media icons and viral sensations like food critic Keith Lee and Tabitha Brown practice group economics when they use their massive platforms to generate support for local businesses, increasing sales for the companies. Brown's segment of Very Good Mondays, where

she highlights small businesses and her followers flood them with support, is an incredible example of virtual collectivism. Lee's restaurant reviews are so powerful, they have a name: the "Keith Lee Effect." Small businesses have seen sales skyrocket by 40 percent following his "blessing." (The flip is also true!) Other companies like the Black Upstart and Official Black Wall Street have used their digital platforms to harness the buying power of the community.

★ **Cooperatives.** A cooperative is a subtype of group economics. Co-ops are an alternative to shareholder- and proprietor-owned businesses. They are structured so that every member shares equally in the ownership and operation of the business; members also share equitably in the profits (aka reinvesting in local community). In a cooperative, decisions are made by collective voting. One of the main goals of a co-op is economic inclusion, to help the "little player" compete with the big guns and to help local businesses flourish in a landscape cluttered with behemoth corporate and global chains. This local focus is so critical and stands in sharp contrast to traditional for-profit chain businesses, in which a large portion of any money you spend there goes to investors and owners. If those folks don't live locally (and they often don't), those profits permanently exit the community—they aren't reinvested in neighborhood shops or nonprofits or restaurants or public projects. Long term, this siphoning of profits can lead to unemployment and a higher rate of poverty.

Co-ops have been around for decades. Civil rights leader and former sharecropper Fannie Lou Hamer was able to sustain Black Mississippi farmers using the co-op model during the years when land was being stripped away from individual Black farms. Hamer, one of my personal heroes, started a 680-acre cooperative farm in the late 1960s called

Freedom Farm, which helped Black farmers in the Mississippi Delta continue farming. Her co-op also included a food store, a boutique, and a sewing enterprise, along with two hundred units of low-income housing. Today, her co-op, now the Federation of Southern Cooperatives Land Assistance Fund, supports dozens of rural farms in six states with a goal of land retention for Black farmers.

There are different types of cooperatives—consumer, business, employment, housing, utility, agricultural, credit unions, banking, and residential. Co-op residential buildings, such as those that have been flourishing in New York City since the 1800s, sometimes offer a more affordable option compared to purchasing a home or condo, since residents share the costs of maintenance. Co-ops also have the ability to reach scale—you've likely heard of some large co-ops, including REI, Ace Hardware, and Ocean Spray. In 2017, there were 64,017[*] businesses in the United States that self-identified as co-ops across four sectors: commercial sales and marketing and production; financial services; social and public services; and utilities. Collectively, they generate more than $600 billion in revenue and account for more than 2 million jobs.

⋆ **Social entrepreneurship.** The term "social entrepreneurship" is relatively new, even though the concept of combining making money with doing good has been around for ages. A social entrepreneur embraces the tenets of entrepreneurship with a mission of creating equity for an underserved population. Their ventures are designed to make a profit, but the mission of disrupting capitalism is as important as

---

[*]  This number is from a 2017 project at the University of Wisconsin–Madison, which is no longer in operation; it reflects the most recent data available for the number of US cooperatives. The USDA puts the number at 30,000 as of 2008.

generating income. We need more creative minds to build in this purpose-plus-profit way. My friend Angel Gregorio, whom I introduced in chapter 2, is a social entrepreneur, operating her membership-based Spice Suite in Washington, DC, with village values and a purposeful approach to closing the racial wealth gap. At her newest venture, Black and Forth, a commercial strip-mall space in a high-rent neighborhood that she purchased for $1 million, Angel has developed a beautiful hub, offering storefront space to Black female entrepreneurs at a reduced cost. The Spice Girls, as she calls them, have an opportunity to be opened for businesses at an affordable price. Black and Forth also features a Black farmers' market, pop-up opportunities, and workshops for young students.

I am also blown away by the work of Nashlie Sephus, PhD, a former computer engineer who is creating a technology hub, the Jackson Tech District, in downtown Jackson, Mississippi. Dr. Sephus, who sold a start-up to Amazon, is pouring her profits into a venture that will elevate Black technology entrepreneurs and reinvigorate a part of her hometown that had fallen into disrepair. Transforming the twelve-acre area into a commercial and residential hot spot, she is fully on assignment to help the next generation stay competitive and prosperous in the STEM sector.

Another inspirational business leader who has amassed wealth and used it to advance opportunities for Black businesses is Atlanta philanthropist and commercial real estate developer Lecester "Bill" Allen. In 2021—exactly one hundred years after the Tulsa Street Massacre—he opened the New Black Wall Street Market, a 125-million-square-foot market space inside a redeveloped Target featuring more than a hundred Black-owned shops and restaurants. The shop owners are offered space at a lower-than-average rent—a key strategy for narrowing the racial wealth gap—and have access to training sessions on marketing, advertising, and online sales support through the Allen Entrepreneurial Institute.

* **Nonprofits.** The role of nonprofits is so important in closing the wealth gap because they are able to allocate *all* their money (minus overhead costs) to the mission. They are agile, able to respond quickly to emerging needs on the ground because they are in daily contact with the community they are serving. They also have the ability to partner with large corporations to fast-track the mission's impacts. Nonprofit founders do not need to have already opened a for-profit business in order to launch a nonprofit. However, when this is the case, entrepreneurs can deepen the impact of their for-profit venture. I founded my nonprofit, Our Village United, so that we could go deeper and offer more comprehensive programming, technical assistance, mentorship, and grants to the businesses in the Village. There are so many incredible nonprofit foundations working in their purpose and lifting the village. To name a few that are doing pivotal work: Young, Black and Giving Back fuels other Black-led nonprofits, helping them fundraise. This is so critical because research shows that Black-led nonprofit organizations operate with lower budgets and have a tougher time securing funding from major institutions than white-led organizations. Dr. Sephus also founded a nonprofit, BeanPath, to bring technology help services and training to the local community and to help bridge the Black-white tech talent gap by offering STEM programs (coding, robotics, 3D printing, AI) and scholarships. (Black people are underrepresented in the technology sector, making up just 8 percent of employees.)

There are other village-minded economic models to consider— microfinance, community land trusts (check out Africatown in Seattle for a robust and exciting model)—so this is far from a complete list. Each of these models aims to position Black businesses to operate within an intentional, equitable community. Only when success is woven into the village and benefits the whole community is it strong enough to continue to power the change that is needed.

## THE VALUE OF AN ABUNDANT MONEY MINDSET

If you have a complicated relationship with money, it's challenging to grow a business, let alone create generational wealth. As a Black person in America, it is often difficult to develop a healthy relationship to money. Understandable, right? A money mindset comprises your core beliefs about money and how those beliefs influence your spending and saving behaviors, as well as who you spend time with and what career you pursue. In a capitalist system that does not treat every person or business equitably, warped beliefs about finances and one's value can begin to take over. For example, if you are constantly in debt because you are subject to high-interest loans and your income doesn't allow you to pay down the balance, you may start to believe that you are a poor manager of money. Or if you were taught that money should not be discussed because doing so is crass or opens you up to criticism, you may be fearful of learning about it or being transparent about your financial situation. Or if you were taught to flaunt money or expensive clothes and jewelry, you may unconsciously value money above other things in life, even when amassing these things doesn't fulfill you. If you grew up in poverty—as nearly 20 percent of Black people do—you may fear taking financial risks because you don't ever want to be poor again, or you may think you are not deserving of making a good living. You may even start to feel shame or discomfort if you *do* begin to make a good living. Or you may feel fear, worrying that your business is built on luck and that your luck will eventually run out. This is a common theme in the vulnerable conversations I have with my friends who are first-generation founders. We recount many moments where we've restricted our most joyous moments and played down our wins because we feared that the success won't be sustained; this is largely due to feeling unworthy and the sheer newness of being successful. On the flip side, if you grew up financially comfortable, you may falsely believe the narrative that people who are on financial assistance are lazy, not trying hard enough, or are seeking a handout. (The reality: Public assistance is essential in a capitalist system where the minimum wage is not truly livable.) You might also erroneously think that race is a determinant of financial class because of false stereotypes. Case in point: The poster child for the welfare recipient is most often a Black person, when in fact government assistance such as SNAP (food stamps) supports more white people than Black people.

I bring up these truths to bust some of the false stories we tell ourselves, as well as to get us thinking and talking about money and our beliefs about ourselves as they correlate to our worth. If a village is going to come together to improve its well-being and future, to close the generational wealth gap, villagers must be able to discuss issues of economics openly and honestly. We cannot create what we cannot say. Doing a deep dive into your money mindset is an important part of the self-exploration every village member should be doing in order to find—and stay—in their purpose. I believe so strongly that our beliefs about finances can either enhance or stifle our businesses and the community that we offer entrepreneurs in the Village a series called Money Mindset, run by a therapist. Untangling a person's relationship with money can help keep villagers focused on communal goals and values as opposed to engaging in financial practices that place profit as the highest goal. Plus, it helps to dismantle some of the guilt and shame that naturally come up when discussing it.

For as long as I can remember, my money mindset has been this: *Money is important because it can help fulfill your goals, but it is not the most important thing.* Although my dad talked to my siblings and me about maintaining good credit, my parents never talked to us about *making* a lot of money. They didn't really address it as good or bad. What they stressed was independence and self-determination. They talked to us about being good people, about having integrity and principles. When I left home, I was able to support myself by following my goals and purpose—teaching—and making a living doing what I loved. When I shifted to becoming an entrepreneur, I saw money as a necessary means to bringing my vision to life.

I now have discretionary income, something my parents did not have at my age. It allows me to donate to community causes I care about—the unhoused population, food insecurity, education. It enables me to take my beloved nephews on vacation, simply because it brings us joy. You should never have to feel defensive about your hard work; you deserve to experience happiness. That said, these vacations also happen to expand my nephews' learning experience; in seeing new places, the boys are exposed to all the options they have before them. (I may not be a teacher anymore, but some tendencies just stick.) Making a good living has also enabled me to purchase investment properties, which I hope to pass down to my nephews one day.

Discretionary income has made it possible to support my grandmothers, and donate to a number of worthy causes, including political candidates. My income has also allowed me to practice group economics in my own business investments. I recently invested in my friend Eunique's company, Happy Hues, and purchased a commercial property with two friends, Jewel and Tracey. Our aim is to house headquarters space for each of our businesses and to offer the space to other founders and creatives—at low-barrier cost— for content creation, events, and more. Despite having done a lot of self-reflection on my own money mindset, there are moments when I feel uncomfortable that my life is far different from those of many in my family. I use these feelings as a reminder to always be mindful that much of my life is a bubble, and I make sure that I walk outside it to know that we have not arrived as a people, that the fight for economic justice and liberation is far from over. One of the ways I fight for that financial freedom is to pay forward what I have learned, to empower my friends and family, and to offer the members of Our Village United, the Village Market, and the Village Retail financial classes and counseling, whether with successful entrepreneurs who have scaled, accountants, wealth-building consultants, or banking professionals. Often, these conversations go beyond the numbers and uncover deep-seated ideas about money—how we value or don't value our talents and what might be thwarting our personal and financial growth.

Several years ago, I met with a business owner in Atlanta named Sam, a divorced single mother of one with a seemingly thriving business. But when we sat down to talk, she looked at me with desperation. "I'm embarrassed to say, I have no idea how to manage the finances of my business," she said. "To be honest, I'm not sure if I'm doing really well or if I'm a total mess." I asked Sam if I could take a look at her books and she begrudgingly agreed as long as I promised not to judge her. She explained that while she has always believed in herself and had no doubt that her business was viable, no one ever talked to her about finances or how to properly build her business in a way that would make it sustainable and strong. When it came to the finances, she said, she was pretty much just "winging it."

I reassured her that everything I've learned has been through trial and error (a lot of error) and no honest entrepreneur, especially those of us without legacy business owners in our families, could say that they had not, at some point, been "winging it." We laughed. She pulled up her QuickBooks and timidly shared her screen with me. What I saw was a business with a great deal of potential but a business model that needed to be refined to ensure that it could scale. For one thing, she charged too little for her services, and her overhead did not support her financial growth. When I challenged Sam to charge more, she balked, worried about what the community would think of her for raising her prices. I looked her in the eyes, nodded to convey my complete understanding, and then asked her directly the following questions: Do you provide a worthy product with stellar customer service? Do you want to continue to be in business? Do you want to pay your staff more? Don't you feel you deserve that? She acknowledged that she did. After a lot of emotional pushback, much of it around fear of judgment, failure, and even a deep fear of growth, we refined her business model. After a few months of implementing these changes, Sam's sales began to surge. She hired more staff and was able to move her office to a beautiful, highly sought-after new location.

Like Sam, many of the members of the Village, particularly those who participate in our business incubator ELEVATE, need a space to be vulnerable and admit that they feel shaky around issues of money. They need the affirmation that *it is OK to make money*. And sometimes it's even more complicated. Sometimes doing what's necessary to scale—like knowing their worth, charging what they deserve, saving more, or reinvesting profit back into the company for necessities for growth—can spark feelings of fear, guilt, and shame. So much of a person's attitude toward money is wrapped up in how they were raised or messages they've been fed based on race or gender. I often ask the businesses in the Village: If you received $10 million today, how would you feel? Would you freak out because you feel undeserving? Or would you get to work because you have a plan? Would you embrace the financial boost and the responsibility that comes with it, or would you feel guilty? There's never only one answer—just imagining the scenario brings up a tangled web of emotions.

Black people have a wealth of emotional experiences around money, some that come from guilt, scarcity, and mere survival over several generations. Generational trauma (or intergenerational trauma) from hardships that our parents, grandparents, and great-grandparents (and great-great-grandparents) experienced—not having enough money to eat three square meals a day, having to rely on public assistance (which people feel ashamed about even when they shouldn't), not being able to afford electricity, having creditors hound you for late bills—get passed down in the way of behaviors and mindsets. Whatever the triggers are, you may have habitual behaviors, feelings, and mindsets—some unconscious—that arise around money and worth. As I shared in earlier chapters, our mindset is key. It's important to do the work to identify our relationship with money and past or present traumas; it's equally important to offer compassion to yourself as you shift your mindset around worthiness (because you are worthy of all things good) and extend forgiveness if your relationship with money has led you to make decisions that you regret. We are all learning and evolving and figuring out how to exist. It's natural and common to feel vulnerable around finances. And *never* feel like a lack of knowledge equates to a lack of worth. You must value yourself before others can value you, and it is your responsibility to the village to hold yourself in high esteem. Similar to self-care, becoming financially literate and honing your money mindset is something you do for yourself and the community.

As we build our legacies, we must change our relationship with money. We must embrace approaches that use wealth building as a vehicle for empowerment, not as an end in and of itself. The vision for the economic future of the Black community is not to simply create more Black millionaires and billionaires who adopt the same principles of a modern capitalist. As journalist Aaron Ross Coleman wrote in *The Nation* (in discussing historian N.B.D. Connolly's book *World More Concrete*): "Black entrepreneurs are capable of inflicting the same racialized inequality seen in the broader American economy as anyone else." The vision is that we build enterprises that advance our communities. During a conversation with my friend Omar Ali, a successful businessman and budding developer in Atlanta, he asked me where I see my family and our community two hundred years from now. Admittedly, before I ever contemplated this question, I had envisioned only what I wanted for my nephews; I did not think about their children's children's children. Now, I intentionally think forward several generations, thanks to him and the Highland Project. I think of myself as but one chapter in a village-made success story, and thanks to the chapter I add, my nephews—and I pray their children's children—will flourish and be able to write their own success stories, and so on and so on. The village only gets bigger. That should be our collective goal. It takes intention, a shift in mindset, and strategic planning—pulling together futurists, builders, enthusiasts, collaborators, and observers—to make this happen. And perhaps most importantly, it takes action. In order for us to experience a different reality, we are not only required to be different and think differently, but we must *act* differently as well.

## Reflection Questions

* What is your one-to-three-year wealth-building strategy for yourself and your family?

* What is your two-hundred-year legacy vision for yourself and for the community?

* What changes do you need to make to put your plans in motion?

* What practices do you have in place in your business that allow for profit but not at the expense of your people?

* How do you currently invest in or collaborate with Black businesses? If it has been a while, what's holding you back?

* How can you practice group economics with your friends, family, or community—is there land for sale or a building that you'd like to purchase?

* What is your relationship to money? Do you feel you deserve to make money?

* When you think about asking for a raise or charging more for your services, how does it make you feel? Why?

* Who taught you about money as it relates to being successful, and what did they say? Do you agree or disagree with their opinions?

* What examples did you see growing up as it relates to managing money?

* What is your biggest fear about becoming financially successful?

# EIGHT

# Support Is a Verb

WHEN I WAS IN THE THROES OF BUILDING UP THE VILLAGE MARKET, I was also in search of a motto, something that would immediately telegraph our mission. I knew that I wanted my motto to signal my values—expanded opportunities for Black entrepreneurs, communal prosperity—and the word "support" kept coming to my mind. And not just support as a vague concept but as concrete action. A verb. *Support Is a Verb.* It felt right—inclusive, action oriented, and village minded. It's a living, breathing slogan, a state of mind and a call to action.

Everything around us—the chair you're sitting on, the car you're driving, the store you just shopped at—is here because someone envisioned it and took steps to make it real. Recently, I was rereading my old journals and flipped to a page where seventeen-year-old me had written in cursive: "I want to open many businesses, travel the world, and teach." I smiled at the younger version of myself for having the ability to envision something vastly different from what I'd experienced. What lay between my teen dreams and my current reality? A series of intentional actions that landed me here. I feel immense pride when I tell my seventeen-year-old self, "We are doing the things we dreamed."

This is the chapter where we focus on intentional action. Chapter by chapter you have been building your blueprint. All of the exploration and work you've done—in your life and with this book—have led you here. By now, you profoundly understand how fertile the soil is that you are working in, that to build something truly sustainable you must bring in others who are aligned to till the soil with you. Our assignments and purpose connect us with others whose purposes align. You know to allow your unique talents and village-driven values to energize you as you work toward your highest self. You understand the importance of nurturing yourself and your relationships and to hold a mindset of abundance as you strive to build your legacy. There will be challenges at times—many of which stem from systemic and historical inequities—but we know that when we lean into the village, we can overcome barriers and rise together. You are ready.

People sometimes ask me, "How do you know when it's time to act?" For me, it's about clarity. Even if the vision isn't fully processed, I have clarity on what I want and how I want to feel throughout the process and when it's fully executed. It's a deep knowing, like knowing when you were a kid that you could finally ride without training wheels. You feel confident in your ability, and, above all, you have peace for what's ahead, even if you do not have all the answers. When uncertainties and questions do arise, you have resolve that you can figure out your next steps. There's an inner push to start building.

I also understand the impulse to want to wait until you've gamed out every possible outcome (planners, I see you!). The ideation phase is important, but you don't want to get stuck in the preparation—and trust me, that's easy to do. A phenomenon called analysis paralysis prevents you from making a decision or acting because you are worried you haven't thought through all the permutations and accounted for every possible error. If this is you, ask yourself, "Am

I procrastinating out of fear? Am I waiting for it to be perfect? Am I doubting that I'm capable?" Remind yourself that when you are in your purpose things have a way of flowing and you will attract the support you need. There's a guiding light that comes from operating in your purpose; you attract other like-minded individuals who serve as lights for your path. You have a village to lift you. Reach out to your ecosystem, ask for help and feedback, lean on your enthusiasts and observers, and address your insecurities by asking the hard questions. Invite in other futurists and experts to lend advice. You no longer have to prove yourself alone.

Despite village support and being on the right path, there will be days of doubt, moments that require you to tap into faith and purpose. Wrestling with doubt is normal, especially for entrepreneurs who are building differently from the norm. But you cannot surrender to doubt. Confront your insecurities and your worries with your capabilities and with the understanding that you are creating a strong village. When you are committed to building equitably, you may encounter more resistance than normal, which in turn requires more fortitude and laser awareness of your purpose and mission. Often, I have been the only person in the room who raises her hand to say, "Why don't we consider doing this a different way?" My advice is to learn to sit with the disquiet and interrogate it. Let it flow in, identify it, and let it flow out so it does not take up residence in your spirit. The more you become comfortable with discomfort, the easier it is to discern when something is fear based or when something is truly off and requires a pivot. Maybe you are about to sign your first lease, acquire a property, or make your first hire. Perhaps you are entering a partnership with a new person or company or taking on a new role. Often, the feeling of unease or anxiousness is simply because the next step is an unfamiliar one. That doesn't necessarily mean it's the wrong path. This is when I encourage the entrepreneurs I work with to trust the process, trust the people you have attracted, and trust your internal signal—your gut. Trust the preparation you've done to reach this point.

I'm sharing nine village verbs and calls to actions that will guide you forward, wherever you are on the spectrum of readiness. These are the ones that I've found deliver the most positive impact for myself and my village as I build. Some of these actions may seem, at first glance, soft or even passive, but that is not the case. There is great power in "quiet" acts, especially when they are practiced faithfully. Just like the unseen supporters holding up the pedestal of a leader, "subtle" actions have tremendous strength and purpose. All of these verbs are meant to move you deep into *the doing*. Each one is meant to be activated *with* and *for* the community.

# VILLAGE VERBS

1. **Lock in.** Your vision is unique and belongs to you and the villagers who are aligned with your purpose. When you commit to your vision, it cements and reinforces your mission no matter what is happening around you. You cannot get distracted by what other people or companies are doing, comparing yourself to others on social media or IRL. Locking in protects your decision-making, helping you say yes to things that will advance your purpose and no to things that are opposed to it. Not every invitation is meant to be met with a yes, but keeping your eyes on *your* prize will help you figure out whether there is some value to be found in the opportunity. Your yes to invitations should be driven by alignment rather than fear of not being in the room. You do not want to be in every room—you want to be in the right room.

   Locking into your vision also means that you and your village can build with a clear sense of what your end goal is.

One of my favorite movies is *Field of Dreams*. I was just eight years old when it came out, and I watched it over and over. The line "if you build it, they will come" stuck with me. The main character was receiving messages to build a baseball diamond, and he didn't understand why. But he (and eventually his village of believers) followed the directives anyway and created something meaningful for the community. In the end, people did come and the community was revitalized. I build with this mindset. My job, your job, is to build with an awareness and assurance that *your* people will come. Being a village-minded entrepreneur requires this level of mental discipline and confidence in what you are creating. You must act according to your ultimate vision even if you don't know how it is all going to happen.

From day one, I built my nonprofit, Our Village United, with a clear goal that we would become a national organization. I locked in. I knew that I would serve entrepreneurs in many cities and states, though I frankly didn't know how and when. But I understood that at the right time it would happen; I just had to start laying the groundwork. As early as 2017, I worked with a consultant to understand the steps it would take to reach my end goal of becoming a 501(c)(3) nonprofit. He taught me the essentials, from structuring a board to compliance to fundraising. Four years after I formed Our Village United in 2020, we were serving more than seven hundred entrepreneurs in twenty-five states and had awarded more than $800,000 in grants. I had a strong belief that my job was to build, that entrepreneurs would find us, and that, city by city, the village would expand. And because that belief was coupled with intentional actions—researching and consulting my village—it became a reality.

> ## TO DO:
> Allow yourself to dream B-I-G with your purpose as your guide. What does the big-picture version of your vision look like and feel like? How can you lock into that now? Write down the steps you can take toward that goal, giving yourself reasonable deadlines.

2. **Show up and connect.** To be in a relationship with good people who are values aligned is a gift. And you can't meet these good people unless you are showing up—literally, in a space of connection (an event, a Zoom meeting) *and* with an open heart for new relationships. This book is the result of me being open to a new friendship with my (now) dear friend Dr. Joy Harden Bradford and to showing up authentically in our relationship from day one. A few years ago, Dr. Joy invited me to be on her podcast, *Therapy for Black Girls*, to talk about sisterhood and elevating Black women. We'd developed a trust based on a passion for supporting our community through wellness events. That bond, and our comfort in being our true selves in each other's presence, allowed us to have a free and inspirational conversation on the podcast. Dr. Joy's literary agent, Rebecca, happened to be listening and told Dr. Joy, "This woman has books in her." That meant a lot to me—I'd wanted to write books since I was a kid and felt I *did* have books in me, ideas that had been floating around looking for the right time and an outlet. From there, it all clicked, and Rebecca became my agent as well. That safe and purposeful connection to Dr. Joy—and my saying yes to her podcast (assignment!) and showing up fully—is the reason you are holding this book.

Sometimes the depth and purpose of your connections will not be revealed right away. Relationships may unfold slowly and have an impact that stretches beyond your lifetime. My mother worked at Batesville Casket Company, where she met Monique Sneed, the human resources director—and the only Black woman in leadership. Often, my mother came home and talked about how intelligent Monique was and how she'd *tell those white people exactly what she meant*—in a state like Mississippi, this is deemed a sign of unshakable courage and self-assuredness. It wasn't long before they became close confidantes. Monique loved the strength and conviction that my mother possessed and leaned on her as a sister friend and sacred person of protection. My mother looked to Monique's education as a tangible example of what it meant to be Black, educated, and confident and saw in her a freedom that she wanted her daughters to experience. A freedom that she herself longed for. They continued to show up for each other, and soon we all became family. When my senior year rolled around, I was eyeing colleges for a basketball scholarship and was at risk of not having much support from the high school athletic program. My mother, understanding this was a make-or-break moment for me, called Monique to help. Monique had connections at Tougaloo College, told me all about the HBCU, and scheduled a visit for me there. The visit changed my life. Tougaloo set me on the course my mother envisioned for me, one that offered freedom and assuredness. Their ability to show up for one another flowed to me. I became the first HBCU graduate on my mother's side of the family. The connections you build can indirectly impact someone else's life and trajectory as well as your own.

**TO DO:** How can you better show up? Is there a person that you've been meaning to meet with? Set up a meeting ASAP. Invite them to coffee. Organize a Zoom. Put a date in the calendar and keep it. Let the magic of authentic connection unfold.

3.  **Keep learning and hire.** Once you lock in, there will be moments—probably countless moments—of not knowing. I don't mean a lack of faith or inspiration (though you will have days where you need to build yourself up); I mean a lack of knowledge. You will not know all the details of how to build a thing. Each step of growth stretches you to a new level where you must learn even more. I think this is an exciting space to be in. When you are learning something, you possess "beginner's mind," a state of curiosity and intrigue that isn't focused on limitations. As entrepreneurs, we are in a constant state of learning—content management systems, management styles and strategies, new ways to problem-solve—the gamut of things involved in our chosen sector. However, we are conditioned to pretend that we know everything, to be the most confident and brightest in the room. This makes us reluctant to raise a hand and say, "I do not know."

    Embracing not knowing has taught me that I have an unlimited capacity to evolve. I didn't know how to launch a nonprofit, so I studied the sector. I was pretty green when it came to management of a nonprofit, so I took an online course and devoured everything I could find about styles that fit my goals. My learned ability to admit "I don't know" and my desire to know has led me to trust my connections, to seek out and hire brilliant people, to harness community. As I've shared, when I decided to build the Village Retail, I had zero experience with retail or managing an e-commerce site. So I reached out to my ecosystem and through a referral found Deana, who had years of experience with retail corporations. I brought her on as the consultant for marketing and digital support for the Village Retail. Next, I tapped my longtime friend Tracey Pickett, CEO of Hairbrella, to get guidance on our digital and e-commerce strategies. I wanted to soak up as much information as I could, but I also wanted to seek out the best support for this huge undertaking.

One of my best hires is my greatest enthusiast, my big sister, Yolanda. As shared previously, she spent a great deal of time helping me think through what it would take to grow and manage a retail store, since she had spent more than twenty years leading retail companies in different sectors. She supported me while I was interviewing to find a store manager. After many interviews, we were still falling short. One evening I called her. "Yolanda, I believe we cannot find anyone because *you* are the person who is meant to lead this mission." Without any hesitation, she said, "I will gladly do so." One of the things I love about learning and hiring is that they compel *you* to connect and allow others to show up in their gifts. It's a chain reaction of doing.

**TO DO:** Assess your ability to ask for help and your discipline to keep learning. What are one or two things that you are currently managing that you need to delegate by hiring someone to manage them?

4.  **Teach it.** When you get, give. When you learn, teach. One of
    the most meaningful things that we can do in community
    is to share what we know. Teaching is an act of love and a
    privilege. I now spend a great deal of my time teaching other
    entrepreneurs how to establish a supportive culture within
    their team. I also mentor them on how to fundraise and
    perfect their art of storytelling. I love sharing both, as these
    are among my greatest strengths, ones I can model with
    passion and proficiency. Teaching entrepreneurs how to tell
    their founder story and to captivate an audience with their
    unique experiences and their "why" is one of my favorite
    classes, as it helps founders to understand how special they
    are and what sets them apart.

    I understand that as an entrepreneur it's challenging to
    find the time to teach. One way to loosely formalize a culture
    of teaching—to give and get at the same time—is to create
    a microcommunity with other entrepreneurs focused on
    sharing hacks. Each entrepreneur has to identify something
    they bring to the table as a key learning hack and lead a
    session—meeting weekly or bimonthly—on that teaching. It's
    a powerful and impactful use of time.

    > # TO DO: What skill can you offer your
    > community that only you can
    > share and that others can benefit from? What about the
    > way you are existing in the world is a model for someone
    > else? How can you deepen that modeling?

5.  **Govern your words and listen intently.** Our words are
    powerful tools and we can use them to raise up or tear
    down. We've talked a lot about intentionality in this book.

I ask you, with love, to understand the magnitude of your words and allow what you speak to the community to be empowering and constructive. I also challenge you to reserve the same level of care for how you speak to yourself. It's easy to get overwhelmed and be overly critical of yourself, but admitting that it's OK that you don't know something or that you need support will lead you to the tools you need.

Communicating with kindness and honesty to people IRL is incredibly important, and it is especially critical on social media, which has become another form of community for so many of us. It's easy to get into the fray of back-and-forth. But imagine if we governed our every word, allowing what we speak and write on our platforms to serve as medicine rather than poison. You are in a unique position to empower your community with words that are affirmative, authentic, and informative, content that drives us to health and a collective mindset.

There is also incredible power in listening. I have learned many valuable business and life lessons by choosing not to always be the most vocal person in the room. When you show genuine interest, people will speak and trust their own truths, feeling inspired and safe to share what has been tucked inside; many are just waiting for the right listener to ask the right questions. Their response will invariably contain proof of their successes, and when they need it most, you can gently echo it back and remind them of their gifts, their wins, and the supportive village they already have surrounding them. Listening also helps you learn and recognize other people's strengths as you build your village—their stories allow you to know where your two worlds could join together and do something meaningful.

> **TO DO:** Carefully determine how you are showing up on your platforms. Does the perception of your message and brand match your values and mission? Review each post before you send it out, ensuring your words have a positive impact. And have you solicited feedback from your customers? How have you implemented what you've heard?

6. **Pivot.** When I was in high school, I played basketball and my father taught me that one of the best moves for a shooting guard / small forward was the pivot. Imagine the situation: The defense is right on your heels and blocking your view of the basket. There's no way to follow the path you expected. So it's time to pivot. A pivot allows you to change direction and elude the defense, to find a new way to make the shot. Back then, pivoting made me a successful scorer. As an adult, it has made me an even better businesswoman.

   Pivoting is the ability to think critically about change, to allow yourself to be open to that change, and to trust the new direction. It's a powerful and creative action that can get you back on track. Pivoting will open a lane for you, one that's uniquely yours. While creating a vision and pursuing it with faith and trust is vital, I also don't want you to be afraid to shift your plans and pivot as many times as you need to get to your ultimate destination. Pivoting just allows the vision to be clearer. It enables you to experience your growth in ways that you wouldn't normally think about. Many companies started out as something different before pivoting to their current iterations. The major hotel chain Marriott International began as a root beer stand in DC in 1927 by J. Willard Marriott. It was only later that it became a restaurant and expanded to hotel ownership. YouTube, now a content creation behemoth, started as a dating site. Ulysses Lee "Junior" Bridgeman, who began as an NBA player, was able to use his sports earnings to invest in fast-food franchises and build a successful restaurant empire. Despite not being a top earner during his playing days and relatively unknown in the league, he demonstrated a remarkable ability to pivot. Today, he is one of the wealthiest former athletes in America and even acquired *Jet* and *Ebony* magazines.

I shared earlier that I was unsure of where my company would go after the pandemic, but I remember what my father said, that pivoting allows you to see the basket more clearly. By changing my direction, I literally opened the doors to my first retail store and my nonprofit, expanding my work and impact.

> **TO DO:** Can you think of a strategy that has stalled or isn't yielding the results you'd hoped for? What other avenues might you try instead—ones you haven't considered before—to meet your goal? Write down all the people and resources you have available to you and start there.

7. **Vote.** Right after Trayvon Martin was killed in 2012, I began to lose faith in the judicial system. It seemed that the legal system worked for some but largely turned its eye from the many Black bodies like Trayvon (the murders of Sandra Bland, Tamir Rice, Breonna Taylor, and countless others would follow and trigger similar feelings). Trayvon's death shattered my heart and my hope. My naivete made me believe that his murder would actually be deemed a murder, and

that his assailant, George Zimmerman, would spend his life
in prison for taking the life of a young man walking home
with Skittles in his pocket and a hoodie on his head. With
the not-guilty verdict, my belief in America dissipated. I was
disenchanted, removed, and resentful. And so I began to
experience a resistance, a begrudging attitude toward my
place, my fight, and where I should spend my time. Honestly, I
did not know if justice was a real thing and if voting mattered
all that much. It seemed that Black people were in the never-
ending story of how justice fails us. What helped bring me
back were conversations with my friends surrounding the
solutions to injustice, and one of those is to exercise our
right to vote—voting to get better judges, district attorneys,
commissioners, and so on. We talked about how *not* voting is
a vote given away—it is saying yes to the conditions of society
that exclude Black and Brown individuals, women, people with
disabilities, and those who don't have the resources to access
fair representation. It is throwing our hands up and choosing
not to fight back. I have learned to transform the energy of my
anger to fight for change in my community, and I implore you
to take steps to do the same. I got involved in local politics
and championed local candidates—mayors, Stacey Abrams,
city council members in Atlanta, state representatives,
my dear friend Gary Chambers, and many others who ran
on a platform for change. I've joined and supported local
organizations such as Streets Alive, which fought for bike
lanes in Atlanta. I've volunteered for Trees Atlanta, Habitat for
Humanity, and Race2Rebuild, to build homes in New Orleans,
all of which gave my heart what it needed: a healthy place to
redirect my energy.

What I know for sure is that when we sit out elections,
the opposing forces win. When we sit out, there's no

accountability for those in power who make decisions without your interest in mind. When we sit out, seats are filled with people who have zero care about the communities that we live in, the local businesses that are open there, the schools that nurture and protect our children, the after-school programs that lend a sense of safety. When we sit out, elders are forgotten. When we sit out, formerly incarcerated citizens—people who leave prison with gaps in their education and work experience—are discarded. When we sit out, Black and Brown farmers are left behind. When we sit out, rural hospitals close. When we sit out, corrupt judges take seats. When we sit out, the courts become imbalanced and the pendulum of justice swings only to some, abandoning others.

To counter assaults against justice, and our basic rights, we have to take action. It is all too easy to believe that your vote doesn't matter, but when we take on that belief, it's another win for them. My grandmother has a saying: "If voting didn't matter, they wouldn't work so hard to make sure you can't do it."

**TO DO:** Find out when your next local election is, review the candidates and propositions, and identify candidates who align with community-first values. Consider volunteering or donating to these people and causes, and ask friends and family to register (if they haven't already) and to vote early.

8. **Invest in your people and spend locally.** Intentionally spending and investing money in your community keeps money circulating in the community. Forty-eight percent of each purchase at local independent businesses is recirculated

locally, compared to less than 14 percent of purchases at
chain stores. Local spending stimulates economic growth
and job creation—*two-thirds of private sector jobs are created
by independent businesses.* And local businesses pay taxes that
support public services such as neighborhood parks, roads,
libraries, and community programs. It's a direct investment in
the infrastructures within your community. For these reasons,
as an entrepreneur I aim to do business with local companies
that have a community and social impact focus.

I also use my business dollars to support and collaborate
with businesses that are environmentally conscious, practice
ethical labor practices, and offer consistent quality of services,
products, and customer service. Several pieces of art hanging
on the walls of the Village Retail are from a local African
American–owned gallery, ZuCot Gallery, which features
incredible contemporary African American artists. The
shopping bags we use for store purchases and our signage are
created by a local Black female–owned business, Moze Print &
Design. All entrepreneurs should consider weaving "spending
as advocacy" into the business plan, whether it's directly
sourcing supplies from local retailers, feeding staff and
patrons by partnering with local farmers, or decorating their
space with the goods of local artisans. Understanding the
value of your hard-earned money—that it goes deeper than just
the superficial transaction—positions you to be a powerful
and active player in your community.

When it comes to investing—in value-aligned businesses
and in friends' or family start-ups—I firmly believe that it is
not only the dollar amount but also the intention of support
that has an impact. I know this firsthand. One day in the
summer of 2017, a couple months after I launched the Village
Market, my phone kept ringing. It was my cousin Delois,
checking to make sure I was going to arrive at the family

reunion at the agreed-upon time. "Yes, yes, I'm coming, I'll be there," I told her for the third time. As I pulled into the parking lot near the park where we were gathering, I understood the reason for her repeated check-ins. There, above the picnic tables at the pavilion, was a huge banner with my picture and the words "Service Award," along with images of me and the Village Market event. I walked toward my family, smiling from ear to ear in disbelief. They presented me with a check for $1,500 and encircled me—my grandmother, my sister, my cousins, and my dad. "We want you to know that we aren't just supporting you with our words, but we want to show our belief in you by investing in your company," said Delois. Apparently, she had been following my developments on Facebook and shared my progress with the extended family, organizing everyone to contribute. Several generations in my family had come together and generously filled the pot in order to help make my dream a reality. Clearly, it takes much more than $1,500 to grow and scale a business, but what that moment did for me was larger than money. The thoughtfulness and intentionality lifted me while I was climbing, confirming that I was seen and believed in. To this day, it's one of the nicest things anyone has done for me; it reminded me that I was not alone, that I had a whole village behind me.

One of my favorite things about investing and spending locally is the impact that it has on the environment: local homegrown businesses are more likely to source their products locally, which reduces the carbon footprint linked to transportation and distribution. Local nonchain stores and restaurants give the community soul, voice, and major vibes. These places are also wonderful opportunities for relationship building. Think about your favorite local businesses that you frequent and why you keep going back.

Aside from the quality of service and products you love, it's likely the connection with the people who go there and work there. Local businesses like Tassili's Raw Reality, where I get my favorite vegan wrap, are what make my daily life in Atlanta such a joy. From my local grocery store, Sevanada, to my dry cleaner, Highland Cleaners, to Natural Creations Salon—where I've been getting my locs twisted by my loctician of more than ten years, Franz-Che'—to Larayia's Bodega, I know the owners and employees and they know me. There's a sense of home where I spend my money, and I feel very much a part of their fabric and success.

Withholding your spending is also a powerful act of advocacy and protest. In 2018, two Black men were wrongly arrested at a Philadelphia Starbucks and the community responded with a viral #BoycottStarbucks hashtag that became one of the most-used hashtags related to Starbucks, second only to #Starbucks. The boycott demanded accountability and resulted in the company issuing an apology and closing thousands of stores for a day to offer racial bias training to the employees. The Montgomery bus boycott of 1955 is, I believe, one of the most impactful forms of economic protest this country has seen. It reminds us that resistance coupled with economics has the power to change minds, laws, and lives.

Not every purchase will demand intentional spending (or withholding), but imagine how influential we'd become as a mission-aligned collective if we made purchasing decisions that reflect our priorities and values. It takes a conscious decision to resist patronizing only where it's convenient and to purchase from local businesses that are positively contributing to the community and society.

**TO DO:** Identify places where you regularly shop that are not local—perhaps sourcing from an online retailer or a nationwide chain—and research local and/or Black-owned businesses that might fill that role instead. Ask neighborhood businesses you love which local businesses they work with and trust, and begin sourcing and spending your dollars there. A great starting resource: your city's Black chamber of commerce, which has long-standing relationships with many area businesses.

9. **Have fun.** Surprise! This is your bonus verb. Here's the thing: As intentional and urgent and serious as your purpose is, if you do not feel good doing it, if you are not experiencing joy in your evolution, something's amiss. We are meant to celebrate one another, to find lightness and humor, to laugh often, and to love deeply in community.

## YOU'VE GOT THIS

When we do things with the village and for the village, we accomplish great things. My life is a testament to this. I have worked with thousands of founders, and the village effect is now sprawling across the country and internationally. Founders tell me we feel like family; that the experience is unmatched, unprecedented, and life-changing; and that it feels like (and I quote) "a Black utopia." Entrepreneurs experience the village effect not only in how they feel and evolve but also in the metrics—through increased social media engagement and brand recognition, soaring revenue, expanded customer base, new hires, and scaling up. And while media recognition feels great, nothing fills my cup more than the peace and joy I have knowing that I am living within my purpose. Nothing compares to the relationship with the founders I have established, my love for my team, and the pride that I have built a company that centers my staff and their well-being. Nothing compares to the feeling that I have created an on-ramp for my nephews and my family. I feel that the ancestors passed the baton to me, and each day I sprint toward a better future for Black people. And when I get tired? I can rest. It's easier to find a second wind in knowing that I do not sprint alone—I am sprinting alongside a strong village. All of the success and praise garnered is because of my unwavering commitment to the vision, setting clear intentions and my belief in the village.

You can absolutely do the same. You have all that you need within you and around you to succeed. The village is the power source, and we have everything to gain when we stand together. When you live purposefully you will be met with success in some form, even if it takes time—time is a gift. When you pursue goals according to your deeply held values, things will eventually begin to fall in place. This doesn't mean it will be easy, but there will be a sense of ease to it. Do not waste your time pursuing things that are not directly in line with your community-rooted values or that do not align with your life's path. This will eat up valuable time and energy and steal from your joy and peace because you are out of alignment and not moving toward what truly speaks to your soul.

Your action plan isn't only about your business plan. It isn't just about accumulating wealth. This is also a spiritual journey— it's about your whole being and your community's health, which are interconnected. Your daily schedule should include dedicated time to care for yourself and fill your cup. This time will spark you and speak to you. Self-care is a sacred act, one that should be undertaken regularly and in service to you and your village.

Finally, remember that divine assignments may be delivered in small doses. Be mindful of the urgent need to build not just for today but also for the next generation, the next seven generations. Be patient. Incremental growth is powerful. Trust your evolution. There will be some nos along the way. Learn to value them and continue onward so you can meet your yes moments. You are the type of entrepreneur, the type of person, that the world needs. And above all, understand that the progress is in purposeful action. Now go and fly. Just don't fly alone.

# Acknowledgments

Since 2016, I have been on a journey of building a village for Black businesses, but many years before that moment, I was a smiling, bright-eyed little girl from the town of Batesville, Mississippi, who loved running through the woods and who got lost in books. Writers, many of whom I never met, became a part of my own little village as a kid and teen, so thank you, Dr. Maya Angelou, Tina McElory Ansa, James Baldwin, Pearl Cleage, J. California Cooper, Nikki Giovanni, bell hooks, Bernice McFadden, Bebe Moore Campbell, Toni Morrison, Sonia Sanchez, Alice Walker, and many, many others. Your books expanded me; they added feathers to my wings.

To the reader, thank you for choosing this book! You are a part of my village now, and it's my hope that you never feel alone or unseen. Keep building your village. You are loved. You are love.

To my family, thank you for all the prayers and for cheering me on. Thank you for loving me. To my grandmothers, Bobbie and Josephine, y'all are my golden girls. I carry with me all that you faced and sacrificed growing up in Mississippi; I pray this book shows you that it was not in vain. I proudly sit at your feet and glean from your wisdom and your beauty. Thank you both for answering all my questions as I wrote this book. Grandma Jo—thank you for all the years that you said, "Now you know you should write a book one day . . . Have you started writing the book yet?" Every time you affirmed it, you made it so. Thank you for always being my enthusiast and my safe space. Grandma Bobbie—thank you for always making sure I know how much you love and support me and for showing me that your gifts truly make room for you. To my great-auntie Pauline, thank you for always sending me the sweetest, most thoughtful gifts and for letting me know you are praying for me.

Daddy, thank you! Thank you for everything. Thank you for being my family historian for this book and for your vulnerability as you recalled memories. You made this book truer and better. You have always made me better. I only want to make you (and my mama) proud.

To my sister Yolanda, thank you for being the quintessential big sister. I can always count on you to be right by my side and to be my protector. To my brother, Roderick—my basketball, hip-hop, and deep-thought partner, I love you. Whitney, my old-soul baby sister, may you continue to build your village, live purposely, and forge your own path.

To my nephews, Sean, Amir, and Jaxon—when I think of each of you, I simply smile. You are just such beautiful rays of light, you embody such purpose and gifts. You have a strong village who loves you so much. I love being your auntie.

To my entire family, aunties, uncles, cousins, and godsons, I love you all.

To my personal village and my dear friends, thank you for pouring into me, making sure that my cup is filled. I am stronger because of your love, Kecia, Ashley (I wrote my book!!!), Hope, Crystal, Danyel, Tasha, Jessica, Kristie, Jeremy O'Brian, Tina (Tine-Tine), Onaje, Gary, Jameka, Sonovia, Astra, Roz, Chandra Grace, Shiquita, Dr. Crystal, Ayanna, Joy, Jewel, and Tracey. My village is strong.

To Dr. Joy Harden Bradford—thank you for not allowing me to limit my dreams for myself and for being a safe space for me to dream. Thank you for being the embodiment of sisterhood.

To Tabitha Brown—thank you for being my enthusiast and my friend. You constantly speak life into me, and it's always right on time.

To Ranika—thank you for always being there and for your willingness and enthusiasm to hear me read every chapter out loud (over and over again). Thank you for always giving me loving and honest feedback whenever I say, "What do you think about this?" I love you!

To Ashley—you know how long I've wanted to write my first book, and you've been right by my side, cheering me on. Thank you for being such a great friend.

Tougaloo College, my alma mater, thank you for teaching me to operate at the highest of excellence.

To the people who were right by my side in the early days as I dreamed and built the Village—Danyel, Carol, Nadia, Kris, Lakil, Courtney, Sonovia, and Berto, I can never thank you enough for your belief in me, for journeying with me. I could not have built the Village without you.

For my dream team at the Village Market, Our Village United, the Village Retail—iron sharpens iron, and you beautiful people are iron. It's truly an honor to build with you.

To the women who have served as mentors for me: Monique Sneed, thank you for introducing me to Tougaloo College and for always being my cheerleader and advocate. Dr. Miranda Freeman, Dr. Beverly Hogan, and Dr. Candice Love Jackson—Tougaloo College gave me so much, Tougaloo gave me you. Thanks for pouring into me, for seeing me, for loving me. To Cheri Lyons—thank you for always making me feel safe and deeply loved. Dr. Jeanette Francis-Ferris—you came into my life right after I lost my mother; your hugs, guidance, and my meals were always right on time and what my heart needed. You taught me to always have space in my heart for one more. Lequisha "LJ" Johnson, RIP, my dear friend. I keep your beautiful spirit and determination at the forefront of all that I love. Rhonda Leland, you've been in my life since I was a teenager and have constantly encouraged, supported, and loved me. I love you. Mrs. Effie Sledge, I can never thank you enough for seeing something special in thirteen-year-old me and for providing me with a safe space. Laura Boughton—thank you for always keeping your classroom door open for tenth grade me. Thank you for every great book you loaned me and for expanding my worldview. I love you all.

To the men who have shown up in my life to protect and propel me: Edgar Holman and Dr. Ashley Hosey, thank you for seeing me, for supporting me, and for opening doors for me. Dennis Hoskins, you've known me since I was an early teen, and you've supported me ever since. Thank you for your heart and for always believing in me. Bradley Durant, thank you for always being there anytime I call you for advice and guidance. You are a great man, and I am sincerely grateful for you. Sterling Dunkley, thank you for always checking in, for encouraging and celebrating me. You know exactly when I need to be uplifted.

To my therapist, Thandi—you know the tears I've cried and the joy I've felt writing this book. Thank you for keeping my heart safe. Thank you for embodying gracefulness and for walking so beautifully in your purpose and gifts. I pray that everyone who embraces therapy has the privilege of working with someone like you.

Thank you to everyone who has advocated for me, ensuring that my work existed in rooms that I was not in. You have made the Village stronger.

I am an embodiment of God's grace and love. I thank God for trusting me to be a vessel. Thank you for protecting and propelling me. Thank you for the strong village you built for me.

Thank you to everyone who has prayed for me, encouraged me to write my first book, and acted as an enthusiast and connector—your love and good energy lift me.

To my literary agent, Rebecca—we did it! Thank you for seeing me and being on this journey with me. Thank you for believing in the Village.

To my editor, Anna: Thank you for recognizing the importance of the work and the importance of the Village. Thank you for asking good questions, for nudging, for pushing me. I value your support.

Tula, we've been in lockstep. I could not have written this love offering without you. I've enjoyed our many conversations, how we do not settle until we've gotten the best out of every sentence and every idea. Thank you for believing in this book, my vision, and the Village. Thank you for your diligence and for being a model professional in your craft and in your gift. You are my village now and I am yours.

Thank you to the teams at Dey Street Books and HarperCollins Publishers for your diligence and belief in this body of work.

To every business who has engaged with the Village through our many programs at Our Village United, the Village Retail, or the Village Market events: I've only wanted you to have a safe space to dream, to grow, to stumble, to be seen, to be loved. I pray you continue to attract and build your village.

I want to acknowledge every student I've taught and every student whose soul has transitioned to the next realm; I love you. You are my students forever, and I pray you are building your village strong.

I want to acknowledge every builder who is on the front lines fighting for Black businesses, for our community—your work is not in vain. May purpose bind you to the work and continue to connect and propel and strengthen the village.

Lastly, I close with the greatest thanks to my ancestors: I follow in your footsteps. Thank you for making sure that the path was made clear, for the love and intentions that you faithfully sacrificed for, for the trees you planted and the shade we sit under because of you. I honor you in all that I do. I honor you in all that I am. Thank you for my crown. Thank you for *our* crown. The village will take it from here.

# Bibliography

## INTRODUCTION

American Independent Business Alliance. "The Local Multiplier Effect." Accessed May 10, 2024. https://amiba.net/project/local-multiplier-effect/.

Augustus, Imani. "Women Wanted: The Equity Gap in Venture Capital." Third Way, March 22, 2022. https://www.thirdway.org/report/women-wanted -the-equity-gap-in-venture-capital.

Baboolall, David, Kelemwork Cook, Nick Notel, Shelley Stewart, and Nina Yancy. "Building Supportive Ecosystems for Black-Owned US Businesses." McKinsey Institute for Black Economic Mobility, October 29, 2020. https://www.mckinsey.com/industries/public-sector/our-insights/building -supportive-ecosystems-for-black-owned-us-businesses.

Black Wall Street USA. "Ottawa W. Gurley." Accessed May 9, 2024. https:// blackwallstreet.org/owgurley.

Brooks, Gwendolyn. "Paul Robeson." Academy of American Poets, accessed May 12, 2024. https://poets.org/poem/paul-robeson.

Center for American Progress. "Poverty in the United States: Explore the Map." Accessed May 12, 2024. https://www.americanprogress.org/data -view/poverty-data/poverty-data-map-tool/.

Edwards, Elizabeth. "Check Your Stats: The Lack of Diversity in Venture Capital Is Worse than You Thought." *Forbes*, February 24, 2021. https://www.forbes.com/sites/elizabethedwards/2021/02/24/check-your -stats-the-lack-of-diversity-in-venture-capital-is-worse-than-it-looks /?sh=c2000ea185de.

Elliot, Debbie. "How a Mule Train from Marks, Mississippi Kicked Off MLK's Poor People Campaign." *Weekend Edition Sunday*. NPR, May 13, 2018. https://www.npr.org/2018/05/13/610097454/how-a-mule-train-from-marks -miss-kicked-off-mlks-poor-people-campaign.

Hepner, Jelia. "Once-Thriving Black Wall Street in Durham Legacy Endures Today." WRAL News. Accessed May 12, 2024. https://www.wral.com

/story/once-thriving-black-wall-street-in-durham-legacy-endures
-today/21036175/.

King Center. "The King Philosophy—Nonviolence." Accessed May 12, 2024.
https://thekingcenter.org/about-tkc/the-king-philosophy/.

Kokalitcheva, Kia. "Taking Stock of Black Venture Capital Dollars." Axios,
February 25, 2023. https://www.axios.com/2023/02/25/venture-capital
-funding-blacks.

Mississippi Blues Trail. "Highway 61 Blues." Accessed May 12, 2024. https://
msbluestrail.org/blues-trail-markers/highway-61-north.

Noel, Nick, Duwain Pinder, Shelley Stewart, and Jason Wright. "The Economic
Impact of Closing the Racial Wealth Gap." McKinsey Institute for Black
Economic Mobility, August 23, 2019. https://www.mckinsey.com/industries
/public-sector/our-insights/the-economic-impact-of-closing-the-racial
-wealth-gap.

Perry, Andre M., Hannah Stephens, and Manann Donoghoe. "Black Wealth Is
Increasing, but So Is the Racial Wealth Gap." Brookings, January 9, 2024.
https://www.brookings.edu/articles/black-wealth-is-increasing-but-so-is
-the-racial-wealth-gap/.

Rice, Solana, Dominique Derbigny, and Lebaron Sims. *Advancing Collective
Prosperity through Entrepreneurship in Atlanta*. Prosperity Now, December
2017, 1–22, 5. https://assets.aecf.org/m/resourcedoc/ProsperityNow
-Advancing_Collective_Prosperity-2017.pdf.

Ryssdal, Kai. "Poverty-Stricken Past and Present in the Mississippi Delta."
*PBS NewsHour*. PBS, July 22, 2016. https://www.pbs.org/newshour/show
/poverty-stricken-past-present-mississippi-delta.

Tell, Dave, and Davis Houck. "Mound Bayou." Emmett Till Memory Project.
Accessed May 9, 2024. https://tillapp.emmett-till.org/items/show/10.

Tippet, Krista. "We Are the Beloved Community." Interview with John Lewis.
*On Being*, July 5, 2016. https://onbeing.org/programs/beloved-community
-john-lewis-2/.

Wexman, Olivia B., and Arpita Aneja. "Beyond Tulsa: The Historic Legacies
and Overlooked Stories of America's 'Black Wall Streets.'" *Time*, updated
May 29, 2021. https://time.com/6050811/tulsa-black-wall-street/.

## CHAPTER 1: THE MYTH OF SELF-MADE

Angelou, Maya. *Our Grandmothers*. New York: Limited Editions Club, 1994.

Asante-Muhammad, Dedrick, Chuck Collins, Josh Hoxie, and Emanuel Nieves.
*The Road to Zero Wealth*. Prosperity Now, September 2017, 1–34. https://
prosperitynow.org/files/PDFs/road_to_zero_wealth.pdf.

Atlanta Wealth Building Initiative. "The Beloved Economy: The Imperative to Build Black Wealth Manifesto." Accessed May 9, 2024. https://www .atlantawealthbuilding.org/the-beloved-economy-the-imperative-to-build -black-wealth-manifesto.

Black Wall Street USA. "Ottawa W. Gurley." Accessed May 9, 2024. https:// blackwallstreet.org/owgurley.

Browley, Jasmine. "Robert Smith's Latest Deal Just Made Him $4.6 Billion Richer." *Essence*, July 11, 2023. https://www.essence.com/news/money -career/robert-f-smith-ibm-vista-equity-partners/.

Bundles, A'Lelia. *On Her Own Ground: The Life and Times of Madam C. J. Walker*. New York: Scribner, 2001.

Chow, Andrew R. "Issa Rae and Hollywood's Unkept Promises." *Time*, February 1, 2024. https://time.com/collection/closers/6564918/issa-rae -hollywoods-unkept-promises/.

Davis, Marcia. "An Interview with Oprah Winfrey." *Washington Post*, September 15, 2016. https://www.washingtonpost.com/lifestyle/magazine /an-interview-with-oprah-winfrey-i-come-as-one-but-i-stand-as-10000 /2016/09/14/25f34b94-4a11-11e6-bdb9-701687974517_story.html.

Evans, Farrell. "How Richelieu Dennis Is Using Venture Capital and Entrepreneurial Smarts to Help Others Create Billion-Dollar Black Companies." *Inc.*, February 23, 2024. https://www.inc.com/farrell-evans /richelieu-dennis-venture-capital-entrepreneurial-smarts-billion-dollar -black-companies.html.

"Famous Musicians: Jay-Z." Biography, updated May 12, 2021. https://www .biography.com/musicians/jay-z.

Gamboa, Glenn. "How Rihanna Turned Everything Upside Down with New Album, 'Anti.' *Chicago Tribune*. Accessed May 9, 2024. https:// digitaledition.chicagotribune.com/tribune/article_popover.aspx?guid =8e62ae8f-7de1-4e7c-b1ac-f464ddf1d7b9.

Gates, Bill. "What I Loved About Paul Allen." *Atlantic*, October 16, 2018. https://www.theatlantic.com/ideas/archive/2018/10/bill-gates-what-i-loved -about-paul-allen/573217/.

Giving Pledge. Pledge Signatories. Accessed May 9, 2024. https://givingpledge .org/pledgers.

Hazzard, Kevin. *American Sirens: The Incredible Story of the Black Men Who Became America's First Paramedics*. New York: Hachette Books, 2022.

Heynan, Nik. "Bending the Bars of Empire from Every Ghetto for Survival: The Black Panther Party's Radical Antihunger Politics of Social Reproduction and Scale." *Annals of the Association of American Geographers* 99, no. 2 (2009): 402–22. https:// doi.org/10.1080/00045600802683767.

Jay-Z, *Decoded*. New York: Spiegel & Grau, 2010.

Kristof, Nicholas. "Pull Yourself Up by Bootstraps? Go Ahead, Try It." *New York Times*, February 19, 2020. https://www.nytimes.com/2020/02/19 /opinion/economic-mobility.html.

Lowe, Turkiya. "Mary Ellen Pleasant (1814–1904)." BlackPast, January 30, 2007. https://www.blackpast.org/african-american-history/people-african -american-history/pleasant-mary-ellen-1814-1904/.

Luxenberg, Steve. "The Forgotten Northern Origins of Jim Crow." *Time*, February 12, 2019. https://time.com/5527029/jim-crow-plessy-history/.

McIntosh, Kriston, Emily Moss, Ryan Nunn, and Jay Shambaugh. "Examining the Black-White Wealth Gap." Brookings, February 27, 2020. https://www .brookings.edu/articles/examining-the-black-white-wealth-gap/.

Moten, Crystal Marie Moten. "Pennies and Nickels Add Up to Success: Maggie Lena Walker." Smithsonian National Museum of American History Behring Center, February 27, 2020. https://americanhistory.si.edu/explore /stories/pennies-and-nickels-add-success-maggie-lena-walker.

NOVA Science Now. "Everyday Examples, Emergence." Accessed May 9, 2024. https://www.pbs.org/wgbh/nova/sciencenow/3410/03-ever-nf .html.

O'Driscoll, Bill. "At Freedom House, These Black Men Saved Lives." NPR, September 27, 2022. https://www.npr.org/2022/09/27/1124161896/at-freedom -house-these-black-men-saved-lives-paramedics-are-book-topic.

Perry, Tyler. "Madea Honored the Strong Black Women I Grew Up With, but It's Time to Move On." *New York Times*, February 28, 2019. https://www .nytimes.com/2019/02/28/movies/tyler-perry-madea.html.

Rice, Solana, Dominique Derbigny, and Lebaron Sims. *Advancing Collective Prosperity through Entrepreneurship in Atlanta*. Prosperity Now, December 2017, 1–22, 5. https://assets.aecf.org/m/resourcedoc/ProsperityNow -Advancing_Collective_Prosperity-2017.pdf.

Ryan, Eric. "How the Godfather of Black Entrepreneurs Is Closing the Racial Wealth Gap—One Billion-Dollar Exit at a Time." *Forbes*, October 3, 2023. https://www.forbes.com/sites/cereal-entrepreneurs/2023/10/03/how-the -godfather-of-black-entrepreneurs-is-closing-the-racial-wealth-gap---one -billion-dollar-exit-at-a-time/?sh=419aac784d99.

Santavirta, Severi, Tomi Karjalainen, Sanaz Nazari-Farsani, Matthew Hudson, Vesa Putkinen, Kertuu Seppälä, Lihua Sun, et al. "Functional Organization of Social Perception Networks in the Human Brain." *NeuroImage* 272, May 15, 2023. https://doi.org/10.1016/j.neuroimage.2023.120025.

Tell, Dave, and Davis Houck. "Mound Bayou." Emmett Till Memory Project. Accessed May 9, 2024. https://tillapp.emmett-till.org/items/show/10.

Virginia Department of Historic Resources. "Jackson Ward Historic
District." Accessed May 9, 2024. https://www.dhr.virginia.gov/historic
-registers/127-0237/.

Young, Kerri. "Landmark Tuesdays: Mary Ellen Pleasant Memorial Park."
SF Heritage, February 2, 2021. https://www.sfheritage.org/community
/landmark-tuesdays-mary-ellen-pleasant-memorial-park/.

## CHAPTER 2: DISCOVERING YOUR PURPOSE
## AND GETTING INTO ALIGNMENT

Alimujiang, Aliya, Ashley Wiensch, Jonathan Boss, Nancy L. Fleischer, Alison
M. Mondul, Karen McLean, Bhramar Mukherjee, and Celeste Leigh
Pearce. "Association Between Life Purpose and Mortality Among US
Adults Older Than 50 Years," *JAMA Network Open* 2, no. 5 (2019): e194270.
https://doi.org/10.1001/jamanetworkopen.2019.4270.

Bates, Karen Grigsby. "Muhammad Ali and Malcolm X: A Broken Friendship,
an Enduring Legacy." *Code Switch*, NPR, February 25, 2016. https://www
.npr.org/sections/codeswitch/2016/02/25/467247668/muhammad-ali-and
-malcolm-x-a-broken-friendship-an-enduring-legacy.

Byng, Rhonesha. "Entrepreneurial Grit: Stacey Abrams Is Not Giving Up in the
Race for Governor of Georgia." *Forbes*, November 5, 2018. https://www
.forbes.com/sites/rhoneshabyng/2018/11/05/how-stacey-abrams-turned-a
-failed-company-into-an-opportunity-for-others/.

Dodds, Frances. "Big Businesses Take Forever to Pay Their Small Suppliers.
These Founders Did Something About It." *Entrepreneur*, March 2024.
https://www.entrepreneur.com/growing-a-business/these-founders-help
-small-suppliers-get-paid-quicker-from/470341.

Dorsey, Corinne. "D.C. Spice Shop Owner Creates Affordable Spaces for Black
Businesses." *Washington Post*, July 31, 2023. https://www.washingtonpost
.com/dc-md-va/2023/07/31/black-and-forth-spice-suite-angel-gregorio
-black-businesses/.

Fonrouge, Gabrielle. "Venture Capital for Black Entrepreneurs Plummeted
45% in 2022, Data Shows." CNBC, February 2, 2023. https://www
.cnbc.com/2023/02/02/venture-capital-black-founders-plummeted
.html.

Fullilove, Michelle. "The World's Community Organizer." Brookings,
September 18, 2010. https://www.brookings.edu/articles/the-worlds
-community-organizer/.

Greater Good Science Center. "What Is Purpose?" *Greater Good*. Accessed
May 9, 2024. https://greatergood.berkeley.edu/topic/purpose/definition.

Heater, Brian. "Stacey Abrams CoFounded Fintech Company, Now Raises $9.5M." TechCrunch, June 9, 2021. https://techcrunch.com/2021/06/09/stacey-abrams-cofounded-fintech-company-now-raises-9-5m/.

Kovaleski, Serge. "Obama's Organizing Years, Guiding Others and Finding Himself." *New York Times*, July 7, 2008. https://www.nytimes.com/2008/07/07/us/politics/07community.html.

Marco, José H., and Sandra Alonso. "Meaning in Life Buffers the Association Between Clinical Anxiety and Global Maladjustment in Participants with Common Mental Disorders on Sick Leave." *Psychiatry Research* 271 (January 2019): 548–53. https://doi.org/10.1016/j.psychres.2018.12.027.

Martin Luther King, Jr. Research and Education Institute. "Montgomery Bus Boycott." Stanford University. Accessed May 9, 2024. https://kinginstitute.stanford.edu/montgomery-bus-boycott.

Muhammad Ali Center. "Meet Ali." Accessed May 9, 2024. https://alicenter.org/meet-ali/.

NAACP. "Martin Luther King, Jr." Accessed May 9, 2024. https://naacp.org/find-resources/history-explained/civil-rights-leaders/martin-luther-king-jr.

Poetry Foundation. "Maya Angelou." Accessed May 9, 2024. https://www.poetryfoundation.org/poets/maya-angelou.

Rotherberg, Emma. "Stacey Abrams." National Women's History Museum, March 2021. https://www.womenshistory.org/education-resources/biographies/stacey-abrams.

Sone, Toshimasa, Naoki Nakaya, Kaori Ohmori, Taichi Shimazu, Mizuka Higashiguchi, Masako Kakizaki, Nobutaka Kikuchi, Shinichi Kuriyama, and Ichiro Tsuji. "Sense of Life Worth Living (Ikigai) and Mortality in Japan: Ohsaki Study." *Psychosomatic Medicine* 70, no. 6 (July 2008): 709–15. https://doi.org/10.1097/PSY.0b013e31817e7e64.

Stuart, S. C. "AfroTech Focuses on Entrepreneurs with a Different Story to Tell." *PCMag*, August 21, 2019. https://www.pcmag.com/news/afrotech-focuses-on-entrepreneurs-with-a-different-story-to-tell.

Theoharis, Jeanne. "The Rebellious Life of Mrs. Rosa Parks: Claudette Colvin." Center for Humanities, Graduate Center, CUNY. Accessed May 9, 2024. https://rosaparksbiography.org/bio/claudette-colvin/.

Tindle, Hilary, MD. *UP: How Positive Outlook Can Transform Our Health and Aging.* New York: Hudson Street Press, 2013.

## CHAPTER 3: ROLL CALL: BUILDING YOUR VILLAGE

Andre Dickens for Atlanta. "About Mayor Andre Dickens." Accessed May 9, 2024. https://andreforatlanta.com/about/.

Bunch, Riley. "Front-Runners Take Hits During Tense Atlanta Mayoral Candidate Debate." Georgia Public Broadcast, October 13, 2021. https://www.gpb.org/news/2021/10/13/front-runners-take-hits-during-tense-atlanta-mayoral-candidate-debate.

Fox, Margalit. "Maya Angelou, Lyrical Witness of the Jim Crow South, Dies at 86." *New York Times*, May 28, 2014. https://www.nytimes.com/2014/05/29/arts/maya-angelou-lyrical-witness-of-the-jim-crow-south-dies-at-86.html.

Li, Wanqing, Xiaoqin Mai, and Chao Liu. "The Default Mode Network and Social Understanding of Others: What Do Brain Connectivity Studies Tell Us." *Frontiers in Human Neuroscience* 8 (2014). https://doi.org/10.3389/fnhum.2014.00074.

NinaSimone.com. "Nina Simone: An Artist's Duty Is to Reflect the Times." https://www.ninasimone.com/biography/.

Norwood, Arlisha R. "Maggie Lena Walker (1864–1934)." National Women's History Museum, 2017. https://www.womenshistory.org/education-resources/biographies/maggie-lena-walker.

Pierpont, Claudia Roth. "A Raised Voice." *New Yorker*, August 3, 2014. https://www.newyorker.com/magazine/2014/08/11/raised-voice.

Poetry Foundation. "James Baldwin." Accessed May 9, 2024. https://www.poetryfoundation.org/poets/james-baldwin.

———. "Maya Angelou." Accessed May 9, 2024. https://www.poetryfoundation.org/poets/maya-angelou.

Shofty, Ben, Tal Gonen, Eyal Bergmann, Naama Mayseless, Akiva Korn, Simone Shamay-Tsoory, Rachel Grossman, Itamar Jalon, Itamar Kahn, and Zvi Ram. "The Default Network Is Causally Linked to Creative Thinking." *Molecular Psychiatry* 27 (2022): 1848–54. https://www.nature.com/articles/s41380-021-01403-8.

Smithsonian National Museum of African American History and Culture. "'A Writer Is by Definition a Disturber of the Peace'—James Baldwin." Accessed May 9, 2024. https://nmaahc.si.edu/explore/stories/writer-definition-disturber-peace-james-baldwin.

Zweig, Jason. "The Daughter of a Slave Who Did the Unthinkable: Build a Bank." *Wall Street Journal*, updated September 25, 2020. https://www.wsj.com/articles/the-daughter-of-a-slave-who-did-the-unthinkable-build-a-bank-11601051297.

## CHAPTER 4: VILLAGE-MADE VALUES

Adams, Desmund. "Harnessing the Power of Diversity for Profitability." *Forbes*, March 3, 2022. https://www.forbes.com/sites/forbesbusinesscouncil

/2022/03/03/harnessing-the-power-of-diversity-for-profitability
/?sh=1a07277e459a.

Bourke, Juliet, Stacia Garr, and 王大威. "Diversity and Inclusion: The Reality
Gap." Deloitte, February 28, 2017. https://www2.deloitte.com/us/en
/insights/focus/human-capital-trends/2017/diversity-and-inclusion-at
-the-workplace.html.

Brewer, Clay. "Servant Leadership: A Review of Literature." *Online Journal
for Workforce Education and Development* 4, no. 2 (Spring 2010). https://
opensiuc.lib.siu.edu/cgi/viewcontent.cgi?article=1008&context=ojwed.

Children's Defense Fund. "Representation Matters: Madam Vice President."
*Children's Defense Fund Blog*, January 20, 2021. https://www.childrensdefense
.org/blog/madam-vice-president-representation-matters/.

Perry, Andre M., Manann Donoghoe, and Hanna Stephens. "Closing the
Black Employer Gap: Insights from the Latest Data on Black-Owned
Businesses." Brookings, February 15, 2024. https://www.brookings.edu
/articles/closing-the-black-employer-gap-insights-from-the-latest-data
-on-black-owned-businesses/.

Quantum Workplace. *2022 Organizational Culture Research Report*, May 4, 2022.
https://marketing.quantumworkplace.com/hubfs/Marketing/Research
/2022%20Organizational%20Culture%20Research%20Report.pdf.

## CHAPTER 5: MANAGING THE HARD STUFF

Aschburner, Steve. "Coronavirus Pandemic Causes NBA to Suspend Season
After Player Tests Positive." NBA, March 12, 2020. https://www.nba.com
/news/coronavirus-pandemic-causes-nba-suspend-season.

Childers, Chandra. "Rooted in Racism and Economic Exploitation: The Failed
Southern Economic Development Model." Economic Policy Institute,
October 11, 2023. https://www.epi.org/publication/rooted-in-racism/.

Daoud, Adel. "Unifying Studies of Scarcity, Abundance, and Sufficiency."
*Ecological Economics* 147 (May 2018): 208–17. https://doi.org/10.1016
/j.ecolecon.2018.01.019.

Dweck, Carol. "What Having a 'Growth Mindset' Actually Means." *Harvard
Business Review*, January 13, 2016. https://hbr.org/2016/01/what-having-a
-growth-mindset-actually-means.

Frady, Marshall. *Martin Luther King, Jr.: A Life*. New York: Penguin, 2005.

Gladwell, Malcolm. "Complexity and the Ten-Thousand-Hour Rule." *New
Yorker*, August 21, 2013. https://www.newyorker.com/sports/sporting
-scene/complexity-and-the-ten-thousand-hour-rule.

———. *Outliers: The Story of Success*. New York: Little, Brown, 2008.

HBR Editors. "How Companies Can Profit from a 'Growth Mindset.'" *Harvard Business Review*, November 2014. https://hbr.org/2014/11/how-companies -can-profit-from-a-growth-mindset.

Intuit TurboTax. "What is the IRS Form 990?" Updated October 19, 2023. https://turbotax.intuit.com/tax-tips/irs-tax-forms/what-is-the-irs-form -990/L4asnXqjZ.

Johnson, Byron, Zakiyyah Brewer, and Julius Hampton. "The Case for Unrestricted Funding for Black-Led Organizations." East Bay Community Foundation, September 26, 2023. https://www.ebcf.org/post/the-case-for -unrestricted-funding-for-black-led-organizations/.

Morrison, Toni. *Song of Solomon*. New York: Vintage Books, 1977.

National Archives, African American Heritage. "The Great Migration (1910– 1970)." Accessed May 9, 2024. https://www.archives.gov/research /african-americans/migrations/great-migration.

Pilgrim, David. "What Was Jim Crow." Jim Crow Museum, updated 2012. https://jimcrowmuseum.ferris.edu/what.htm.

US Bureau of Labor Statistics. 2020 Results of the Business Response Survey. Accessed May 9, 2024. https://www.bls.gov/brs/2020-results.htm.

Wilkerson, Isabel. *Caste: The Origins of Our Discontents*. New York: Penguin Random House, 2020, esp. ch. 16.

———. "The Long-Lasting Legacy of the Great Migration." *Smithsonian Magazine*, September 2016. https://www.smithsonianmag.com/history /long-lasting-legacy-great-migration-180960118/.

## CHAPTER 6: SELF-CARE AND THE WELL COMMUNITY

Beach, Mary Catherine, Somnath Saha, Jenny Park, Janiece Taylor, Paul Drew, Eve Plank, Lisa A. Cooper, and Brant Chee. "Testimonial Injustice: Linguistic Bias in the Medical Records of Black Patients and Women." *Journal of General Internal Medicine* 36 (March 2021). https://doi.org /10.1007/s11606-021-06682-z.

Berg, Sara. "What Doctors Wish Patients Knew About Decision Fatigue." American Medical Association, November 19, 2021. https://www.ama-assn .org/delivering-care/public-health/what-doctors-wish-patients-knew -about-decision-fatigue.

Childs, Emma, and Harriet de Wit. "Regular Exercise Is Associated with Emotional Resilience to Acute Stress in Healthy Adults." *Frontiers of Physiology* 5 (2014). https://doi.org/10.3389/fphys.2014.00161.

DeGruy, Joy. "Post Traumatic Slave Syndrome." Dr. Joy DeGruy. Accessed May 9, 2024. https://www.joydegruy.com/post-traumatic-slave-syndrome.

Deloitte. *Women @ Work 2022: A Global Outlook.* Accessed May 10, 2024. https://www2.deloitte.com/content/dam/insights/articles/glob-175228 _global-women-%40-work/DI_Global-Women-%40-Work.pdf.

Gallup and Workhuman. *Amplifying Wellbeing at Work and Beyond Through the Power of Recognition.* 2022. https://assets.ctfassets.net/hff6luki1ys4 /Qu9UUxsvV9iJyouN23M6t/acf085b6de297317538bd43de686d023/ amplifying-wellbeing-at-work-and-beyond-through-recognition.pdf.

Harvard T.H. Chan School of Public Health. "Diet Review: Anti-inflammatory Diet." Reviewed October 2021. https://www.hsph.harvard.edu /nutritionsource/healthy-weight/diet-reviews/anti-inflammatory-diet/.

Hill, Latoya, Samantha Artiga, and Usha Ranji. "Racial Disparities in Maternal and Infant Health: Current Status and Efforts to Address Them." KFF, November 1, 2022. https://www.kff.org/racial-equity-and-health-policy /issue-brief/racial-disparities-in-maternal-and-infant-health-current -status-and-efforts-to-address-them/.

Jackson, Fatimah, Latifa Jackson, and Zainab ElRadi Jackson. "Developmental Stage Epigenetic Modifications and Clinical Symptoms Associated with the Trauma and Stress of Enslavement and Institutionalized Racism." *Journal of Clinical Epigenetics* 4, no. 2:11 (2018). https://www.primescholars.com/articles /developmental-stage-epigenetic-modifications-and-clinical-symptoms -associated-with-the-trauma-and-stress-of-enslavement-and-instit.pdf.

Jobin, J., C. Wrosch, and M. F. Scheier. "Associations Between Dispositional Optimism and Diurnal Cortisol in a Community Sample: When Stress Is Perceived as Higher than Normal." *Health Psychology* 33, no. 4 (2014): 382–91. https://psycnet.apa.org/doiLanding?doi=10.1037%2Fa0032736.

Lorde, Audre. *A Burst of Light.* Atlanta: Firebrand, 1988.

Lukasik, Karolina M., Otto Waris, Anna Soveri, Minna Lehtonen, and Matti Laine. "The Relationship of Anxiety and Stress with Working Memory Performance in a Large Non-depressed Sample." *Frontiers in Psychology* 10 (2019). https://doi.org/10.3389/fpsyg.2019.00004.

Mende-Siedlecki, P., J. Qu-Lee, R. Backer, and J. J. Van Bavel. "Perceptual Contributions to Racial Bias in Pain Recognition." *Journal of Experimental Psychology: General* 148, no. 5 (2019): 863–89. https://doi.org/10.1037 /xge0000600.

National Institute on Aging. "What Do We Know About Diet and Prevention of Alzheimer's Disease?" Reviewed on November 20, 2023. https://www.nia .nih.gov/health/alzheimers-and-dementia/what-do-we-know-about-diet -and-prevention-alzheimers-disease.

Perzichilli, Tahmi. "The Historical Roots of Racial Disparities in the Mental Health System." American Counseling Association, May 2020. https://

www.counseling.org/publications/counseling-today-magazine/article
-archive/article/legacy/the-historical-roots-of-racial-disparities-in-the
-mental-health-system.

Raza, Zara, Syeda F. Hussain, Victoria S. Foster, Joseph Wall, Peter J. Coffey, John F. Martin, and Renata S. M. Gomes. "Exposure to War and Conflict: The Individual and Inherited Epigenetic Effects on Health, with a Focus on Post-Traumatic Stress Disorder." *Frontiers of Epidemiology* 3 (2023). https://doi.org/10.3389/fepid.2023.1066168.

Rogers-LaVanne, Mary P., Alyssa C. Bader, Alida de Flamingh, Sana Saboowala, Chuck Smythe, Bernadine Atchison, Nathan Moulton, et al. "Association Between Gene Methylation and Experiences of Historical Trauma in Alaska Native Peoples." *International Journal for Equity in Health* 22 (2023). https://doi.org/10.1186/s12939-023-01967-7.

Scott-Jones, Gwendolyn, and Mozella Richardson Kamara. "The Traumatic Impact of Structural Racism on African Americans." *Delaware Journal of Public Health* 6, no. 5 (November 2020): 80–82. https://doi.org/10.32481/djph.2020.11.019.

Thevanes, N., and T. Mangaleswaran. "Relationship Between Work-Life Balance and Job Performance of Employees." *IOSR Journal of Business and Management* 20, no. 5 (May 2018): 11–16. https://www.iosrjournals.org/iosr-jbm/papers/Vol20-issue5/Version-1/C2005011116.pdf.

US Department of Health and Human Services Office of Minority Health. "Mental and Behavioral Health—African Americans." Accessed May 9, 2024. https://minorityhealth.hhs.gov/mental-and-behavioral-health-african-americans.

US Department of Veteran Affairs, Office of Research & Development. "Study Finds Epigenetic Changes in Children of Holocaust Survivors." VA Research Currents, October 20, 2016. https://www.research.va.gov/currents/1016-3.cfm.

World Health Organization. "Burn-Out an 'Occupational Phenomenon': International Classification of Diseases." May 28, 2019. https://www.who.int/news/item/28-05-2019-burn-out-an-occupational-phenomenon-international-classification-of-diseases.

## CHAPTER 7: GENERATIONAL WEALTH AND PATHWAYS TO PARITY

Albuquerque, Daniel, and Tomer Ifergane. "The Racial Wealth Gap: The Role of Entrepreneurship." London School of Economics, March 23, 2023. https://www.lse.ac.uk/CFM/assets/pdf/CFM-Discussion-Papers-2023/CFMDP2023-10-Paper.pdf.

Annie E. Casey Foundation. "What Is a Social Enterprise?" *Casey Connects* (blog), December 10, 2020. https://www.aecf.org/blog/what-is-a-social-enterprise.

Baboolall, David, Kelemwork Cook, Nick Notel, Shelley Stewart, and Nina Yancy. "Building Supportive Ecosystems for Black-Owned US Businesses." McKinsey Institute for Black Economic Mobility, October 29, 2020. https://www.mckinsey.com/industries/public-sector/our-insights/building -supportive-ecosystems-for-black-owned-us-businesses.

Britannica Money. "Capitalism." Accessed May 10, 2024. https://www.britannica .com/money/capitalism.

Brown, Jan Shelly, Matthew Finney, Mark McMillan, and Chris Perkins. "How to Close the Black Tech Talent Gap." McKinsey Institute for Black Economic Mobility, February 3, 2023. https://www.mckinsey.com/bem /our-insights/how-to-close-the-black-tech-talent-gap.

Carr, Teneshia. "Inside This Amazon Scientist's $25 Million Plan to Turn 12 Abandoned Acres in Jackson Mississippi into a Tech Hub." *Inc.*, February 23, 2021. https://www.inc.com/teneshia-carr/nashlie-sephus-jackson -mississippi-bean-path-tech-hub.html.

Chaia, Alberto, J. P. Julien, Lucy Pérez, Duwain Pinder, Shelley Stewart III, Dominic Williams, and Nina Yancy. "Mapping the Road to Prosperity and Parity for Black and Latino Residents Across America." McKinsey Institute for Black Economic Mobility, March 15, 2024. https://www .mckinsey.com/bem/our-insights/mapping-the-road-to-prosperity-and -parity-for-black-and-latino-residents-across-america?cid=other-eml-mtg -mip-mck&hlkid=84f1e8b924824acd832cedbe654ead5a&hctky=1926&hdpid =1e7886f0-05e7-4532-b337-0c3c8fe0f62f#interactivemap.

Coleman, Aaron Ross. "Black Capitalism Won't Save Us." *The Nation*, May 22, 2019. https://www.thenation.com/article/archive/nipsey-killer-mike-race -economics/.

Connolly, N. B. D. *A World More Concrete: Real Estate and the Remaking of Jim Crow South Florida*. Chicago: University of Chicago Press, 2014.

Cooperative Development Institute. "What's the Difference Between Cooperatives and Collectives?" February 13, 2015. https://cdi.coop/coop -cathy-coops-and-collectives-difference/.

Curtis, Tiffany. "How Generational Trauma Affects Your Finances and How to Heal." NerdWallet, November 2, 2022. https://www.nerdwallet.com /article/finance/generational-trauma.

Davis, Calandra, and Sara Miller. "A Dream Deferred: The Lasting Legacy of Racist Redlining in Mississippi and the Deep South." *Mississippi Free Press*, April 8, 2021. https://www.mississippifreepress.org/11089/a-dream -deferred-the-lasting-legacy-of-racist-redlining-in-the-deep-south.

Desilver, Drew. "What the Data Says About Food Stamps in the U.S." Pew Research Center, July 19, 2023. https://www.pewresearch.org/short-reads/2023/07/19/what-the-data-says-about-food-stamps-in-the-u-s/.

Desmond, Matthew. "In Order to Understand Capitalism, You Have to Start on the Plantation." *New York Times*, August 14, 2019. https://www.nytimes.com/interactive/2019/08/14/magazine/slavery-capitalism.html.

Elliott, Jessica. "How to Set Up a Profit-Sharing Program at Your Company." US Chamber of Commerce, November 29, 2022. https://www.uschamber.com/co/run/finance/setting-up-profit-sharing-programs.

Elmi, Sheida, and Bianca Sofia Lopez. "Foundations of a New Wealth Agenda: A Research Primer on Wealth Building for All." Aspen Institute, December 2021. https://www.aspeninstitute.org/wp-content/uploads/2021/11/ASP-FSW_FoundationsNew-WealthAgenda_120121.pdf.

Fairlie, Robert W. "The Impact of COVID-19 on Racial Disparities in Small Business Earnings." US Small Business Administration, Office of Advocacy, August 16, 2022. https://advocacy.sba.gov/wp-content/uploads/2022/08/Report_COVID-and-Racial-Disparities_508c.pdf.

Federation of Southern Cooperatives. *FSC/LAF 2023 Annual Report,* 2023. https://federation.imagerelay.com/share/c62d6b82778d437a9ba7c4a2fbb22f80.

Ford, Tanisha. "Money Behind the Movement." New America, February 14, 2023. https://www.newamerica.org/the-thread/civil-rights-movement-and-money/.

Fortune Business Insights. "Thermos Bottle Market Size, Share & Industry Analysis, By Material (Stainless Steel, Plastic, Glass, and Others), by Application (Household and Commercial), and by Regional Forecast, 2024–2032." April 30, 2024. https://www.fortunebusinessinsights.com/thermos-bottle-market-104435.

Francis, Dania, Darrick Hamilton, Thomas Mitchell, Nathan Rosenberg, and Bryce Wilson Stucki. "How the Government Helped White Americans Steal Black Farmland." *New Republic*, May 5, 2022. https://newrepublic.com/article/166276/black-farm-land-lost-20th-century-billions.

Frank, Robert. "The Wealth of the 1% Just Hit a Record $44 Trillion." CNBC, March 28, 2024. https://www.cnbc.com/2024/03/28/wealth-of-the-1percent-hits-a-record-44-trillion.html.

Gilbert, Jess, Spencer D. Wood, and Gwen Sharp. "Who Owns the Land? Agricultural Land Ownership by Race/Ethnicity." *Rural America* 17, no. 4 (Winter 2002): 55–62. https://www.ers.usda.gov/webdocs/publications/46984/19353_ra174h_1_.pdf.

Gross, Terry. "A 'Forgotten History' of How the U.S. Government Segregated America." *Fresh Air*, NPR, May 3, 2017. https://www.npr.org/2017/05/03

/526655831/a-forgotten-history-of-how-the-u-s-government-segregated
-america.

Harris, Neal, and Gerard Delanty. "What Is Capitalism? Toward a Working
Definition," *Social Science Information* 62, no. 3 (2023). https://doi.org
/10.1177/05390184231203878.

Highland Project. "What We Do." Accessed May 12, 2024. https://www
.thehighlandproject.org/what-we-do.html.

Institute for Policy Studies. "Racial Economic Inequality." Inequality.org.
Accessed May 10, 2024. https://inequality.org/facts/racial-inequality/.

Kroeger, Teresa, and Graham Wright. "Entrepreneurship and the Racial Wealth
Gap: The Impact of Entrepreneurial Success or Failure on the Wealth
Mobility of Black and White Families." *Journal of Economics, Race, and
Policy*, vol. 4 (February, 2021). https://link.springer.com/article/10.1007
/s41996-021-00081-6.

Liberto, Danile. "What Is Capitalism: Varieties, History, Pros & Cons,
Socialism." Investopedia, May 8, 2024. https://www.investopedia.com
/terms/c/capitalism.asp.

Manyika, James, Gary Pinkus, and Monique Tuin, "Rethinking the Future of
American Capitalism." McKinsey. Accessed May 10, 2024. https://www
.mckinsey.com/featured-insights/long-term-capitalism/rethinking-the
-future-of-american-capitalism.

Martin Luther King, Jr. Research and Education Institute. "Our God Is
Marching On!" Stanford University, March 25, 1965. Accessed May 10,
2024. https://kinginstitute.stanford.edu/our-god-marching.

Martin, Roger L., and Sally Osberg. "Social Entrepreneurship: The Case for
Definition." *Stanford Social Innovation Review* 5, no. 2 (Spring 2007).
https://ssir.org/articles/entry/social_entrepreneurship_the_case_for
_definition#.

Michals, Debra, ed. "Fannie Lou Hamer." National Women's History Museum,
2017, https://www.womenshistory.org/education-resources/biographies
/fannie-lou-hamer.

Mosely, Tonya. "How Black Socialite Mollie Moon Raised Millions to Fund the
Civil Rights Movement." Interview with Tanisha Ford. *Fresh Air*, NPR,
October 30, 2023. https://www.npr.org/2023/10/30/1209018407/mollie
-moon-our-secret-society-tanisha-ford.

Moss, Dave. "The Fundraising of Martin Luther King, Jr." Unfunded List,
January 16, 2023. https://www.unfundedlist.com/the-fundraising-of
-martin-luther-king-jr/.

Moss, Emily, Kriston McIntosh, Wendy Edelberg, and Kristen Borady. "The
Black-White Wealth Gap Left Black Households More Vulnerable."

Brookings, December 8, 2020. https://www.brookings.edu/articles/the
-black-white-wealth-gap-left-black-households-more-vulnerable/.

National Association of Consumer Advocates. "Predatory Lending." Accessed
May 10, 2024. https://www.consumeradvocates.org/for-consumers/predatory
-lending/.

National Cooperative Business Association CLUSA International. "ABCs of
Cooperative Impact." Accessed May 10, 2024. https://ncbaclusa.coop
/resources/abcs-of-cooperative-impact/.

Nwanji, Ngozi. "Angel Gregorio Bought a $1M Property to Open a Strip Mall
for Black-Owned Businesses." AfroTech, January 17, 2023. https://afrotech
.com/black-woman-entrepreneur-angel-gregorio-black-and-forth.

Osakwe, Kingsley. "Group Economics (Part 2): Exploring the Models."
*Medium*, June 28, 2023. https://medium.com/@theconnectseries/group
-economics-part-2-exploring-the-models-a930db845199.

Osberg, Sally R., and Roger L. Martin. "Two Keys to Sustainable Social
Enterprise." *Harvard Business Review*, May 2015. https://hbr.org/2015/05
/two-keys-to-sustainable-social-enterprise.

Peek, Sean. "What Is Social Entrepreneurship?" US Chamber of Commerce,
July 30, 2020. https://www.uschamber.com/co/start/startup/what-is-social
-entrepreneurship.

Penrice, Ronda Racha, with additional reporting by Gavin Godrey. "We Took a
Walk Down the New Black Wall Street. Here's What We Learned." Capital B
Atlanta, February 8, 2022. https://atlanta.capitalbnews.org/we-took-a-walk
-down-the-new-black-wall-street-heres-what-we-learned/.

Perry, Andre M., Hannah Stephens, and Manann Donoghoe. "Black Wealth Is
Increasing, but So Is the Racial Wealth Gap." Brookings, January 9, 2024.
https://www.brookings.edu/articles/black-wealth-is-increasing-but-so-is
-the-racial-wealth-gap/.

Perryman, Darrah. "More Than Just a Co-Op: How Cooperatives Strengthen
Economic Power." Blog post. US Department of Agriculture, October 24,
2022. https://www.usda.gov/media/blog/2022/10/24/more-just-co-op-how
-cooperatives-strengthen-economic-power.

———. "National Co-Op Month: How USDA Rural Development Supports
Cooperatives." Blog post. US Department of Agriculture, October 4, 2022.
https://www.usda.gov/media/blog/2022/10/04/national-co-op-month-how
-usda-rural-development-supports-cooperatives.

Pollard, James. "Black Texas Farmers Were Finally on Track to Get Federal
Aid. The State's Agriculture Commissioner Wants to Stop That." *Texas
Tribune*, January 24, 2022. https://www.texastribune.org/2022/01/24/texas
-black-farmers-sid-miller-lawsuit/.

Presser, Lizzie. "Their Family Bought Land One Generation After Slavery. The Reels Brothers Spent Eight Years in Jail for Refusing to Leave It." ProPublica / *New Yorker*, July 15, 2019. https://features.propublica.org /black-land-loss/heirs-property-rights-why-black-families-lose-land -south/.

Scott, Rachel, Briana Stewart, and Gabriella Abdul-Hakim. "Some Black Farmers Worry They Could Be Left Out of Federal Debt Relief Programs." ABC News, May 2, 2023. https://abcnews.go.com/US/black-farmers-worry -left-federal-debt-relief-programs/story?id=98997659.

Smithsonian National Museum of African American History and Culture. "Bayard Rustin." Accessed May 12, 2024. https://nmaahc.si.edu/bayard -rustin.

SNCC Digital Gateway. "Diane Nash." Accessed May 12, 2024. https:// snccdigital.org/people/diane-nash-bevel/.

———. "Ella Baker." Accessed May 12, 2024. https://snccdigital.org/people /ella-baker/.

University of Wisconsin Center for Cooperatives. "2021 Cooperative Governance Research Initiative." April 2024. https://resources.uwcc.wisc .edu/Worker/CGRI_Worker%20Co-op_Final.pdf.

———. "Research on the Economic Impact of Cooperatives." Accessed May 10, 2024. https://reic.uwcc.wisc.edu/summary/.

USDA National Agricultural Statistics Service. *Farms and Land in Farms, 2021 Summary*, February 2022. https://www.nass.usda.gov/Publications/Todays _Reports/reports/fnlo0222.pdf.

## CHAPTER 8: SUPPORT IS A VERB

Alvarez, Lizette, and Cara Buckley. "Zimmerman Is Acquitted in Trayvon Martin Killing." *New York Times*, July 13, 2013. https://www.nytimes.com /2013/07/14/us/george-zimmerman-verdict-trayvon-martin.html.

American Independent Business Alliance. "The Local Multiplier Effect." Accessed May 10, 2024. https://amiba.net/project/local-multiplier-effect/.

Dugandzic, Matthew. "The Story of the Former Milwaukee Buck that Became the Richest NBA Player You Never Heard Of." SI.com, December 11, 2022. https://www.si.com/nba/bucks/old-school/former-milwaukee-buck-that -became-the-richest-nba-player-you-never-heard-of.

Epstein, Ronald, MD. *Attending: Medicine, Mindfulness and Humanity*. New York: Scribner, 2017, esp. ch. 4.

Marriott International. "Our Story of Innovation." Accessed May 10, 2024. https://www.marriott.com/about/culture-and-values/history.mi.

Mitchell, Stacy. "Key Studies: Why Independent Matters." Institute for Local Self-Reliance, January 8, 2016. https://ilsr.org/key-studies-why-local-matters/.

Pathak, Arohi. "Second Chance Policies Help Individuals Leaving Incarceration Build Financial Security." Center for American Progress, April 5, 2023. https://www.americanprogress.org/article/second-chance-policies-help-individuals-leaving-incarceration-build-financial-security/#:~:text=Second%20chance%20policies%20remove%20barriers%20to%20reentry&text=Many%20individuals%20leave%20prison%20with,to%20their%20families%20or%20communities.

Thebault, Reis. "Trayvon Martin's Death Set Off a Movement That Shaped a Decade's Defining Moments." *Washington Post*, February 25, 2022. https://www.washingtonpost.com/nation/2022/02/25/trayvon-martins-death-set-off-movement-that-shaped-decades-defining-moments/.

University of Minnesota Duluth, UMD News Center. "Expert Alert: The Economic Impact of Shopping Local." Interview with Monica Haynes, director, Bureau of Business and Economic Research. November 18, 2021. https://news.d.umn.edu/articles/expert-alert-economic-impact-shopping-local.

US Chamber of Commerce. "The State of Small Business Now." April 10, 2023. https://www.uschamber.com/small-business/state-of-small-business-now.

Zara, Christopher. "Here's How Quickly 'Boycott Starbucks' Spread Across the Internet." *Fast Company*, April 18, 2018. https://www.fastcompany.com/40560741/heres-how-quickly-boycott-starbucks-spread-across-the-internet.

# About the Author

AN AWARD-WINNING EXPERT in education and business development, Dr. Lakeysha Hallmon is the CEO of the Village Market, the Village Retail, and Our Village United, Inc. Hallmon's innovative village model—which helps businesses with big ideas turn them into even bigger profits—has become highly sought-after and has generated $8.3 million in sales for Black businesses. She has been celebrated as one of the Root 100 (most influential Black Americans), one of *Forbes* 50 Culture Champions, an *Atlanta Business Chronicle* 40 Under 40, and one of *Georgia Trend* magazine's most influential business leaders. Hallmon has been featured in *Forbes*, on CNN and the *Today* show, and in *Essence*, among many other outlets. She is a native of Batesville, Mississippi, and currently resides in Atlanta, Georgia.